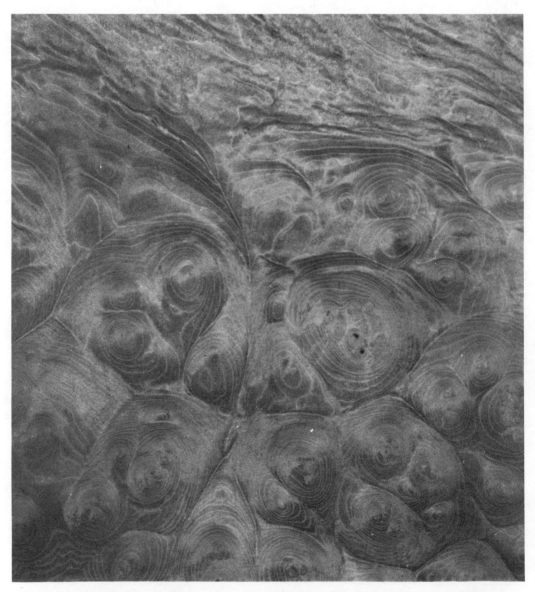

Poplar burl is green, soft sea green, a rare color in veneers. It has another unique characteristic. Its figuration, traced by delicate tan veins, forms into two distinct patterns: a succession of waves called swirl, and circles within circles called burl

Veneering Simplified

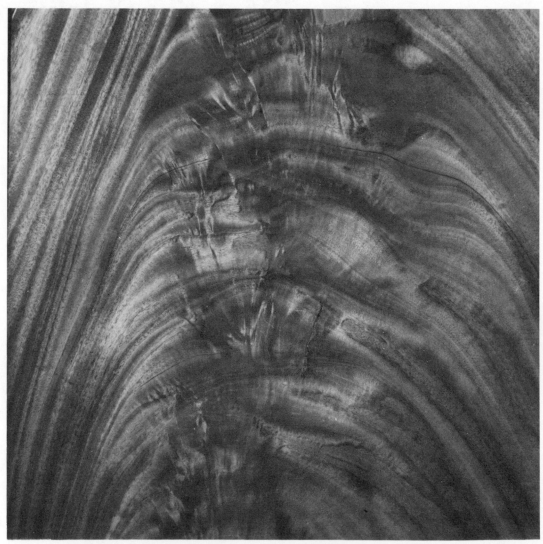

Mahogany crotch is cut from a large tree found in African forests. Unlike most of the exotic veneers, it comes in comparatively large sheets and is reasonably plentiful. The strong coloration of pinkish brown in its pendant plumes comes to a rich, deep-toned reddish brown when it reaches the central staff. It is called by many fanciful names: plume, feather, flame, waterfall, cathedral, and ponytail

Veneering Simplified

Harry Jason Hobbs

CHARLES SCRIBNER'S SONS
New York

ISBN: 0-684-16763-8
Library of Congress Catalog Number: 78-67821

Contents

Continued

How to use *Veneering Simplified*

You will benefit most from this book, at present and in the future, by spending a few minutes now studying the Contents. The Contents was prepared especially to serve as a useful guide to specifics within the subject area.

This approach to a technical book like *Veneering Simplified* is suggested as the quickest way to learn in considerable detail where to locate the specific guidance contained in its 16 varied chapters.

An early understanding of what the book contains will thereafter save considerable time when you are looking for the answer to a problem confronting you.

Materials and tools. Veneers illustrated and described throughout the book have been limited to the finest veneers to work with, and only veneers that are available commercially on the craftsman market. Other materials and tools used in demonstrations were chosen because, in the work experience of the author who used everything shown, they represented the most satisfactory of modern materials and tools for veneering.

Equipment to make. Some of the equipment used in veneering demonstrations was homemade, either because it was cheaper to make than to buy, or because no such product is made for sale. Examples include angle-iron clamping arrangement that cuts your investment in clamps, tin-can alcohol lamp used in repair work, veneer hammer made from a discarded floor buffer, old hacksaw blade for a straightedge, clamping frame from lumber discards to substitute for numerous bar clamps, scratch beader serving as a molding plane with assorted cutters, jointing jig for edging veneer, to name a few. The object of such devices, of course, is to equip you to do successful veneering without suggesting a substantial workshop investment.

Veneer identification. You will find the concentration of aids to identification in chapter 4, including numerous close-up wood grain photographs and a descriptive list of more than 50 popular kinds of veneer. In addition, as you study veneering techniques and follow the photographs showing procedures, you will discover the names of veneers used in the demonstrations, and from this recurring aid you will become acquainted with more of the finest veneers.

Illustrations. With the exception of only a few photographs otherwise credited to outside sources all photography was done by the author especially for this book. The profusion of actual work-in-progress photographs is intended as a picture-course in veneering. From these real-shop photographs you can see which tool does the work, how to hold it, and what it accomplishes.

The reference system of figure numbers in photograph captions and figure numbers in text works this way: the first number indicates the chapter number, and the second number is the rotation number within the chapter. (9-5) means chapter 9, illustration number 5. In a few instances, two or three related photographs belong to one figure number.

Projects to make. Chapter 9 puts technical instruction into action. Appealing projects were created to make use of veneering methods recommended throughout the book. The simplest of all projects, a gift set of coasters, has more to recommend it than may at first be realized. There you see how to select veneer grain to advantage, how to cut veneer, two ways to glue veneer, how to assure glue bond by rollering. Other projects involve three important inlaying techniques simplified by innovative methods. Scanning the pictures in this project section gives you a preview of basic veneering techniques. And while pictures are said to tell more than words, you will miss a lot of know-how if you skip the text.

Where does it lead? What appears in the project section to be an introduction to the simplest of veneering achievements has far-reaching possibilities. The basic skills of handling, selecting, cutting, gluing, clamping, and trimming applied to small projects are the same skills you will need when you undertake more rewarding veneering projects of your own creation.

Acknowledgments

It has been a pleasure and a highly rewarding experience to develop veneering methods and to translate known methods into visual form and step-by-step instructions for this book. To Gertrude M. Constantine, president, Albert Constantine and Son, Inc., who gave me this opportunity and liberally provided veneers, tools, and related materials used throughout the demonstrations, I wish to express my lasting gratitude.

For the use of the few additional photographs needed to add visual explanation to veneering, where as author I was unable to take such photographs, I express my grateful appreciation to companies and associations in the industry:
Adjustable Clamp Company, illustrations 8-3 and 8-4.
Australian News and Information Bureau 3-2.
The Dean Company 3-4, 3-7, 3-9, 3-10.
Fine Hardwoods/American Walnut Association 2-1, 3-3.
Plywood & Panel magazine 3-5, 3-6, 3-8.
United Nations, African sequence, back panel of book jacket.

To Richard Brown my thanks for photographs of Cocker Spaniel and The Old Cowboy, chapter 16. To The New York Public Library my appreciation for their helpful assistance in research.

For the liberal use of information about veneering and for technical data about veneers, manufacturing methods, and materials used in veneering, I am grateful to Borden Chemical. Ted J. Connelly, The Dean Company. Donald H. Gott, Fine Hardwoods/American Walnut Association. Forest Products Laboratory, U.S. Department of Agriculture. The Franklin Glue Company. Clark E. McDonald, Hardwood Plywood Manufacturers Association. James F. Burrell, Plywood & Panel magazine.

For valuable technical assistance my special thanks to members of the staff of Albert Constantine and Son, Inc., Philip Capazzola, Glenn R. Docherty, and James Vignola. To my wife, Mary, my deep gratitude for her enduring patience and assistance during procedural setups for photography, and for so competently handling the production problems involving art and manuscript.

Harry Jason Hobbs

1. Veneering—past, present, and future

For a quick introduction to the physical character of veneer—the natural material of extraordinary, enduring beauty—let us begin with this simple definition. Veneer is a thin sheet of wood. Throughout this book, the demonstrations were performed with two standard thicknesses of veneer, 1/28 and 1/40. These are the two thicknesses you will normally work with.

To give yourself a better understanding of what these trade terms mean, in case you are not already familiar with the difference, you could count 7 sheets of this book. Sheets, not pages. Feel the thickness between your fingers. Seven sheets come approximately to 1/28 inch. Of course the paper will be more flexible than veneer. Count 4 sheets and feel the approximate thickness of 1/40 inch.

Veneer was not always cut so thin, nor so smooth and uniform in thickness. In ancient times it is said that the first veneer was literally shaved from trees after the bark was chipped off. Shaved strips proved to be stronger than bark, and no doubt more interesting, for weaving baskets and making containers.

Stone tools are assumed to have done the stripping. Veneers cut in this manner must have been incredibly thick and irregular. Nevertheless, early man made the first important veneering discovery, that trees harbored material of rare beauty, and that the rich colors and patterns of inside wood varied from tree to tree.

Records from the tombs of ancient Egypt show that the skillful Egyptians practiced the art of cutting thin sheets of fine woods and applying them to wooden objects. Inlaid and veneered chests, tables, cabinets, and burial boxes have been removed from the tombs of the Pharaohs of Egypt. Sealed from the outside world for nearly 3,500 years, a few of these astonishing articles, preserved in museums, testify to a high level of veneering artistry.

One of the major reasons attributed to the advanced culture of the Egyptians, perhaps the chief reason they left richly veneered objects, was their accidental proximity to copper mines. They discovered how to make bronze tools that could hold a fairly sharp edge. With bronze to work with, they made saws. With saws they cut veneer from wood planks which had been cut with bronze adzes. They were able to saw veneers to thicknesses of ¼ inch and somewhat less. They developed hand grinders of stone, and with these implements they could smooth the veneers which had been overlaid as sheets or inlaid as mosaics on treasured objects. Wall carvings and paintings told the cryptographers these facts. These markings and pictures reveal another major advance in the art of veneering. They show Egyptian carpenters squatting at their work tables, spreading glue from a glue pot to a sheet of thin wood.

Although their tools were primitive, the Egyptians produced excellent work and passed on to later civilizations two basic veneering techniques, cutting wood thin and gluing it over common woods as decorative enrichment.

The shortage of fine woods in Egypt was probably responsible for the high level of craftsmanship attained by Egyptian craftsmen. Scarce material demanded careful, skillful handling. Precious woods were brought to Egypt by ship. To make the most of prized logs craftsmen cut them into veneer and laid the veneer on common woods. It is obvious that, in this ancient land, necessity was the patron of veneering. To beautify their surroundings with exotic veneers

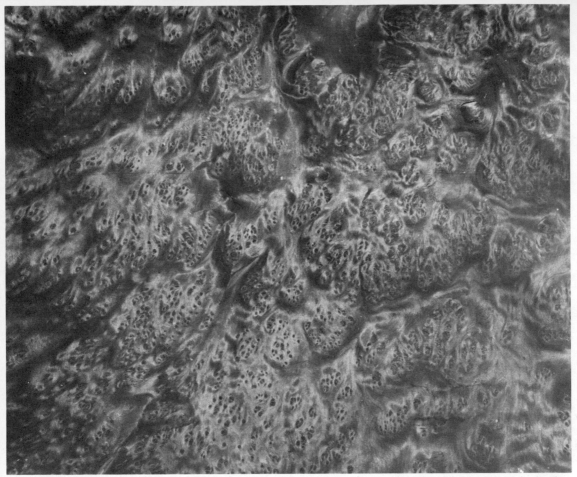

Thuya burl has been a highly-prized wood since the beginning of recorded time. When it was known as thyine wood in the time of King Solomon, it was called "precious wood." In the days of Roman dominance, Cicero owned a valuable table, said to be worth $50,000, the top of which had been veneered with thuya.

In the Atlas Mountains of Algeria, thuya is harvested as a burl from underground roots. In the 19th century, Moroccan natives stole thuya by burning brushfires at night to clear the land so they could dig out the valuable roots.

Thuya is essentially brownish red. Some thuya has a yellowish brown color. Some areas turn almost black. Thuya grain goes in every direction. It twists and swirls its way around numerous burl eyes. Thuya, like most burls, is a delicate wood. It finishes beautifully and is always worth the patience it demands in handling. Crossband veneer must be laid under thuya.

the Egyptians were forced to develop the art of veneering to a high level.

Later civilizations, down through the centuries for 1,500 years, continued the ornamental use of veneers without making any notable contributions to the art of veneering until Roman times. When Rome became a center of power and wealth, costly sheets of veneer were used lavishly as decorative material on room panels, door frames, chests, boxes, and table tops.

The Romans went for veneer in a big way. As a decorative device in earlier civilizations the use of veneer had been limited by manufacturing difficulties. Slow, laborious cutting methods restricted both inlaying and sheet veneering. The Romans vastly improved manufacturing methods. They invented the bow saw. It held a thinner bronze blade and it permitted the blade to turn at an angle so that only the thin blade had to pass through the saw kerf. In other types of frame saws, before and since, the frame that held a non-turning blade had to pass through the kerf. It was wasteful and damaging to the veneer. This great new invention enabled the enterprising Romans to cut thin veneer more efficiently and in wider sheets. The Romans also invented a very creditable hand plane for smoothing and equalizing the thickness of sawed veneer. They replaced the stone hand grinders of the Egyptians with efficient metal scrapers for smoothing and leveling veneered and inlaid surfaces. These new veneering tools brought about a swift revolution in the art of veneering.

In Roman times veneer became one of the early status symbols. Craftsmen were hired by the rich to create wildly exotic patterns of veneer for walls, cabinets, and table tops. Such fanciful conceptions came to be known as "the spots of the leopard, the swarm of bees, the stripes of the tiger."

In the extravagant era of Roman dominance, veneering reached a flamboyant pinnacle, and like the bizarre art of many recorded civilizations, the art of veneering became tiresome and decadent. But before this decline set in, history tells of a costly table of unsurpassed beauty owned by Cicero. The top was veneered with magnificent thuya burl imported from across the Mediterranean, from the land now Algeria. At present currency values this prized table would have been worth $50,000.

Veneering went down with the Romans. Through the dark ages there is evidence of wood inlay but nothing to indicate a significant advance in veneering. As a purely ornamental art it was carried on chiefly by monks who made mosaic inlays for church decoration. In the 15th century more elaborate designs appeared, mainly in Italy. Monastic orders devoted themselves to inlaying designs in a softwood background and they developed a form of veneering related to our marquetry. In the 16th century both the Italians and the Germans introduced figures, scrolls, and landscapes into marquetry work and applied their creations to cabinets, boxes, and furniture. This form of applied pictorial veneering alternately flourished and waned during the next few centuries.

By 1700 another dramatic change in veneering had taken place, having gradually developed in England and throughout continental Europe. Matched veneer panels replaced, for the time, pictorial veneering. Cabinet doors and chest drawer fronts were faced with highly figured veneers. Matched designs became more and more elaborate. Again history was repeating itself. Each craftsman attempted to outdo his forerunner. And again the ornamental use of veneer declined. Revival, in the same form of elaborate matched veneered panels, came back into fashion about 1800.

In 1805 a powered circular saw was invented in England. Though not very successful for cutting veneers, it gave promise that one day veneers could be cut from logs swiftly and uniformly. Seventy-five years later the inventor's dream came true. Powered knife-slicers and powered rotary lathes were successful. Veneering, from then on, was on the march.

At the beginning of our century, veneer was being manufactured in dependable thicknesses, in wide variety, and in larger volume than ever before. Then the biggest advance in the history of veneering took place. Veneers were glued together with the grain of each layer turned at right angles to its neighbor. This notable discovery gave the woodworking world a new product called plywood.

Veneers, only decorative and ornamental until now, suddenly were given structural strength. Veneered panels proved to be stronger than solid wood; more stable than solid wood; and more beautiful than solid wood. For the woodworking industry the future seemed assured, but the craftsman had to wait nearly 50 years before industrial chemists perfected wholly satisfactory glues that could be used successfully for panel veneering under home-shop conditions.

If the present correctly foretells the future, craftsmen are now at the beginning of a new era of veneering. Exotic veneers are readily available. They are thinner, less brittle, more manageable. Modern glues are stronger, faster, cleaner than ever before. Advanced techniques for handling, cutting, gluing, clamping, and even repair, are widely circulated. In the hands of modern craftsmen, so richly equipped, the future of panel and craftwork veneering does, indeed, seem assured.

2. What a few basic veneering skills can do for you

The first reason a woodworker has for turning to veneer is his desire to enrich the visual quality of his work. The second is to improve the structural quality. Veneer, by itself, can contribute the good-looking surface, but to provide structural stability veneer needs backing. Veneer with backing can fill both of the woodworker's desires with consistent dependability and fill both of them better than solid wood.

Panels that are properly veneered do not warp. There is little wonder, therefore, that veneered panels are the number one modern choice over solid wood for cabinet construction, table tops and other broad surfaces, in the furniture industry and in the home shop.

It would be impossible to construct a piece of furniture of highly figured woods, such as burl walnut, because the grain of such wood is produced by disease or accident, and the pieces are quite small. It is structurally weak, extremely brittle when machined, and would split and warp out of shape. Veneer cut from the burl is manageable and of course beautiful. Other woods, particularly tropical varieties as ebony, are so dense that if a piece of furniture were constructed from the solid wood, it would be so heavy as to be practically immovable. Furthermore, the arrangement of pieces of such woods into the intriguing matched patterns you will learn to create with veneers would not be possible. (2-1)

For structural stability the thin sheets of veneer you work with must have backing. Veneer is 1/28 or less in thickness. One sheet is called a single ply. When you glue several sheets together at right angles to each other you have built a plywood panel. (2-2) A plywood board is many times stronger than solid wood of equal thickness. It is less likely to split when being

bored for screws or dowels, and less likely to be broken under blows or stress. Because of its greater strength, plywood construction may be made thinner than solid construction with consequent economy in material. The natural tendency of wood to absorb or give off moisture, according to the varying moisture content of the air, is largely eliminated in plywood construction, because the tendency of any layer to contract or expand is offset by other layers, glued at right angles, with a tendency to move the opposite way.

There are other ways, simpler ways, for you

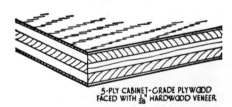

5-PLY CABINET-GRADE PLYWOOD
FACED WITH ⅟₂₈" HARDWOOD VENEER

2-2. Plywood construction. Five veneer sheets crisscrossed and glued together make a balanced 5-ply panel. This is only one of the ways to make veneered panels for your projects

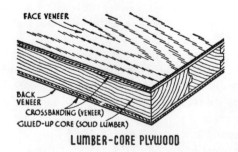

FACE VENEER

BACK
VENEER
CROSSBANDING (VENEER)
GLUED-UP CORE (SOLID LUMBER)

LUMBER-CORE PLYWOOD

Another way to make a 5-ply panel is called lumber core or solid core plywood. Two sheets of crisscrossed veneer go on top and back

2-1. Matched panels are created by edge-joining consecutive sheets of veneer. Top, book-matched figured cherry.
Second from top, 2-piece redwood burl. Above, 2-piece
East Indian rosewood. Top right, mahogany, reverse-
diamond match. American walnut, 2-piece sliced, figured. Bottom right, 4-piece diamond match walnut

to build the veneered panels you need. Sometimes the foregoing plywood construction is the best way to build a panel; sometimes you can follow an easier course. The system of building layer on layer of thin veneer is only one way, and is one of the hardest ways for the home craftsman, although it is the cheapest and most prevailing method in industry. All of the panel options are fully covered in later chapters under the general subject of core construction, for both flat panels and curved panels.

When plywood panels are mentioned, a person generally thinks first of house construction, next of wall paneling, both beyond our scope. The home craftsman is not equipped to build even the smaller sheets used for wall paneling. This book will confine itself to instructions for building all sizes of panels for furniture and craftwork which you are able to build with equipment that can be managed in the home shop. That could mean panels up to about 2 or 3 feet wide and 3 or 4 feet long. Within reasonable limits, the principles explained could be adapted to larger work.

Many uses for panels. Cabinets, wardrobes, chests, desks, home bars, clock cases, table tops and mounting panels for craftwork designs are the popular projects calling for veneered panels today. When you custom-make your own panels, these and many other projects to improve your home are within your abilities. Some of them are remarkable money-savers.

Compare the cost of a readymade hi-fi cabinet with the cost and quality of a cabinet you can

2-3. Veneer makes attractive boxes out of plain basswood boxes bought readymade in craft stores. This one was covered with pale gold avodire mottle veneer. The tiger was cut from Macassar ebony, head from teak, nose from zebrano. Three tiger parts were overlaid on box lid. Inside should be lined

2-4. This was a basswood box bought readymade to hold box of facial tissue. It was veneered with reddish brown makori (African cherry). Decorative border was set in by the simplest of inlaying methods. Chapter 9 gives details for veneering and inlaying box

make. Your cabinet can exhibit really elegant matched-panel doors and fine walnut, teak, or rosewood veneer over the case. All this, compared to the usual cheaper woods of the cabinet you buy.

The many uses you already visualize for veneered panels are just the beginning of your involvement. There are many other rewarding ways to use veneers. Following are a few of them.

Veneered boxes. The universal appeal of small boxes gives the veneer craftsman a standing invitation to use his skill. There is a ready demand in every household for boxes in assorted shapes, sizes, and styles. Hinged boxes, compartmented boxes, loose-lid boxes; long, square, deep and shallow—whatever they are, someone wants them. Uses defy the imagination, but standard purposes include boxes to hold jewelry, playing cards, collectors items, sewing kits, facial tissue, stationery, musical units, desk items, buttons, coins, household cash kitty, and personal treasures of many sorts. (2-3)

You can make your own boxes and then veneer them, but the simplest way to start is to choose what you want from the extensive varieties of readymade basswood boxes now sold by most craft suppliers.

For a demonstration in the craftwork techniques of covering what are usually called craft boxes, a white basswood box for holding facial tissue was purchased and then veneered. (2-4) The top has a slot for pulling out tissue from a standard box of tissue placed inside by removing a slip-out bottom. Chapter 9 shows you how to do the work.

Unpainted furniture veneered. Many department stores and most mail-order catalog houses with household merchandise departments offer a large selection of ready-to-finish furniture. There are nightstands, nesting parson tables, cocktail tables, chests of drawers, desks, vanity stands, and other styles suited to veneering, providing you thoughtfully select suitable construction. (2-5) Square edges on drawer fronts, chest tops, table tops and legs are the features to look for.

Square edges are easiest to veneer. Shaped edges, either rounded or molded, are to be avoided if possible. Even square tapered legs can be veneered, but not turned or shaped legs. A popular style of bandsawed scroll on the lower rail of chests can be veneered. Some curves can be negotiated. The serpentine drawer front of a chest of drawers can be veneered. A bowed

2-5. A plain unpainted chest from department store was upgraded with figured walnut veneer

drawer front, Hepplewhite style, can be veneered. If a table edge is molded and has a square lip at the top, you can veneer the table top up to this square lip and apply matching finish to the molded edge. A table with a shaped edge of this type, even a drop-leaf style, can be veneered even though you cannot veneer the turned legs.

Serving tray. Another example of distinctive things you can make when you apply your veneering abilities is the unusual serving tray illustrated. (2-6) Ordinary serving trays arouse little comment, but the matched panel made for this tray is likely to be admired wherever it is used. The tray illustrates what can be accomplished when you learn the simple techniques of matching veneers.

Beautiful Brazilian rosewood was selected for the demonstration of making a matched panel. Pre-cut walnut tray molding was purchased and required only mitering to fit it around the tray.

The method of joining two nearly identical

2-6. Serving tray. Two sheets of Brazilian rosewood were book-matched at the center to make a veneer face wide enough for this project. Book-matching technique fully detailed in another chapter opens many opportunities in craftwork and cabinetmaking

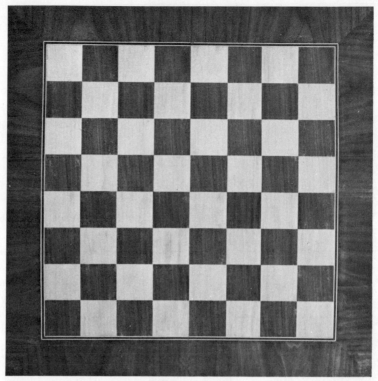

2-7. Chessboard. This simple project was accomplished by gluing the assembled veneer face to an 18-inch square flakeboard panel, and veneering the edges with matching walnut border. Back should be veneered to create warp-free balanced construction

pieces of veneer, easily learned, opens many opportunities to practice one of the more advanced techniques in veneering. Matched veneer panels do more to enrich woodworking projects than almost any other decorative technique you can use.

Instructions given in chapter 7 for making matched panels will equip you to make them for a variety of useful purposes such as cabinet doors, chest drawer fronts, table tops, and other pieces of furniture

Readymade veneer designs. One of the easiest ways to complete a useful project in quick time is to use a readymade veneer face. The illustrated **chessboard** (2-7) is a good example of a popular project that starts with the purchase of an assembled 1/28 veneer chessboard face.

Maple and walnut squares, surrounded by a walnut border, were assembled by the manufacturer. They are held in place by a crisscross of paper tape on one side. The tape, applied on the

face of the veneer assembly, is to be removed after the veneer has been properly glued to a warp-free panel. Step-by-step instructions on this procedure, which applies to all face veneer projects, are given in chapter 9.

Matched faces readymade. A few standard sizes of matched veneer faces are offered by woodworker suppliers. They are 4-piece matches of extraordinary beauty. These faces have been skillfully cut of 1/28 veneer and assembled, with joints taped. They are ready to glue down on any suitable core panel. Readymade matched faces obviously provide the easiest way to make beautiful matched panels. Kinds include diamond-matched walnut, diamond-matched mahogany and reverse diamond-matched mahogany, and swirl walnut. Sizes are 15x30 and 30x30. The smaller size can be cut apart lengthwise, if desired, to yield two drawer fronts. Two faces would provide faces for a 4-drawer chest.

2-8. Fraternal emblems like this are available as pre-assembled veneer faces. Can be mounted on panels as square plaques, or inlaid square or round in table tops

Masonic fraternal emblem. (2-8) This design also is purchased as an assembled veneer face. Gum tape completely covers one side as a means of keeping the many parts of the design in secure position until glued permanently to a panel. Tape is then removed. Instructions in chapter 6. Other fraternal emblems are also available as assembled veneer faces.

The illustrated emblem was mounted on a same-size panel to become a wall plaque. Emblem faces are suited also for use as decorative insets in card-table tops, chests, cabinet door panels, serving trays, and other such surfaces. They may be inset as squares or removed from the outer square and laid as circular designs.

There is an intriguing variety of veneer faces now offered in woodworker catalogs. The list includes complete, matched-face exotic wood assemblies for table tops, from end-table size up to card-table size, square, rectangular and round. There are inlaid initials from A to Z measuring 3 inches in diameter. A regulation size backgammon face; 12 zodiac faces; sportsman's outdoor animals in action; and the list is growing. All of these skillfully made veneer faces are ready for mounting on or in any smooth wood surface. (2-9)

Veneer faces offer all craftsmen a simplified way to enrich woodworking projects with decorative veneers. And to the beginner they offer probably the most reward for the least veneering experience.

Veneer over scarred furniture. Covering scarred furniture surfaces, especially the tops of tables, chests, and desks, with rich-looking veneer sounds like magic, but in reality is one of the most popular modern uses for veneer in the home shop. Besides the obvious improvement such an achievement contributes to home decor, there is a remarkable money-saving benefit. New furniture is expensive. Veneer is not, when you consider the coverage you can get for a moderate investment. For instance, assume that you own a coffee table with a top surface measuring 2x4 feet. Normally this is the hardest working surface in the home and is first to need restoration. At today's prices you can buy figured mahogany, walnut, and many other appropriate woods for approximately four dollars to cover the coffee table. Comparison with the cost of furniture replacement brings many home owners to the same conclusion—that the simple techniques of veneering are worth the learning.

The methods of laying new veneer over old on a flat, smooth surface involve cutting the veneers, probably edge-joining to gain width, gluing, and trimming the edges. These are not difficult operations. Full instructions for every step are included in following chapters.

Low-cost handsome tables. One of the unique advantages of veneer is its ability to turn unusable discards into attractive and serviceable furniture and accessories for your home. There are many examples. One is the little-known old-door trick. A real money-saver.

Locate a hollow-core interior door. It can be used or new. Even new doors are inexpensive when you consider your intended usage. Cover the bland uninteresting Lauan mahogany with an exciting veneer that becomes the decor of your family room, breakfast area, sunroom, study, or wherever you need a table of substantial size. Install readymade legs. Chapter 10 reveals the technical know-how.

2-9. Veneer faces like this sampling of colorful designs provide woodworker with quick way to dress up furniture and craftwork. Side you now see will glue down, gum paper backing will peel off

2-9

3. How veneers are cut so thin

The veneers you are selecting today for your next project started when a wind-blown seed lodged in a favorable spot on the forest floor, or when man planted a seedling for grove cultivation. In the forest this event took place perhaps 100 to 120 years ago. In the grove under watchful cultivation a mahogany seedling may be harvested in 60 years with a trunk diameter of 28 inches. Mahogany trees growing wild in a Central American or African forest normally are not felled until the tree is much larger, often 48 inches.

The veneers you want to use are hardwood veneers. The search for choice hardwood trees in a mixed forest of countless unwanted trees which are too small or of non-marketable varieties exposes foresters to constant danger. Felling trees so that they can be grappled and dragged out of jungles, transporting them over rugged trails, and rafting them down treacherous waterways make stories of high adventure.

For a moment, study the illustrated veneer sample here. (3-1) Notice its engaging interlocked figure, suggesting a basketry weave but called, unromantically, blistered. This is euca-

3-1. Eucalyptus veneer from the world's largest eucalypt forests, Australia. Color is tan to gold with flashes of pink. Figure is known as blistered

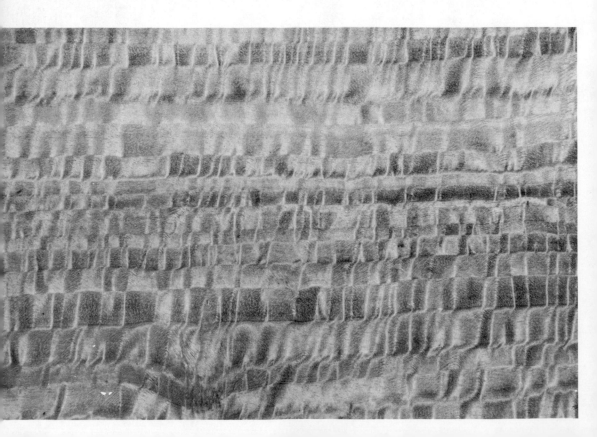

lyptus veneer. Visualize it in full color, an over-all golden hue with brown and pink accents. From now on you are likely to think of it in terms of its origin and the manpower that went into its delivery within your reach.

This piece of veneer came from Australia where the world's great forests of eucalyptus are found. A brief pictorial account of eucalyptus veneer, from forest to sawmill, is shown. (3-2)

Another quick view of the veneer story, this one from Africa, appears on the back panel of the jacket of this book.

There are many unillustrated steps in the cycle from tree to veneer. One major step that cannot be lightly passed is the actual manufacturing process of veneers. In other words, how do they cut veneer so thin?

Nearly every wooded area in the world yields one or more of the 100 to 175 species of trees that come to the United States for manufacture into veneer. Logs are selected for their outside ap-pearance. This is the first of numerous risks the industry must take, from log broker to manufac-turer. Prime logs come normally in whole log form, but in some cases as half logs, and less frequently as roughly squared timbers called flitches.

Prime woods are in such firm demand that prime logs go right into processing. Secondary logs may be stored near the manufacturing plant in a pond until they are needed. Storing in water sounds risky, but it actually preserves the log. Immersion prevents checking and splitting which would occur as the log dries out, and it wards off harmful, hungry insects.

Manufacturing methods, somewhat stan-dardized for many years, are now changing rapidly with a surge of new technology within the industry. Debarking, for example, was commonly performed after soaking. Now the operation has been automated in many modern plants. The huge logs travel along a vicious debarker which strips them clean before they enter the plant. Cleaned logs go to giant band saws where they are trimmed on four sides and have their corners cut off. The squared logs, now called flitches, (3-3) move on. Some varieties, softer, pliable varieties, may now go to cutters. Most flitches, and particularly prime hard-woods, go instead into huge vats of hot water,

3-2. Loggers perched perilously on planks are under-cutting a huge eucalypt. Final sawing from opposite side will fell the tree straight toward the cameraman

Huge felled trees are trimmed of branches, and logs cut to most valuable section before being lashed together for the tractor to drag them toward flatcar loading area

At Australian sawmill acres of eucalypt logs are waiting to enter debarker before going for hot bath for softening and then to veneer slicer

3-3. Hardwood log being squared by band saw. When squared on all sides it becomes a flitch

and often later into boiling water. (3-4)

This bath is the first step in cutting veneer so thin. The bath moistens and softens the flitch for easier cutting to unbelievable tolerances of possibly 1/40, in uniform thickness, in sheets 8, 10, even 17 feet long, slice after slice at a rate of 50 or more sheets per minute; and some machines can operate at 100 strokes per minute.

Without the hot bath, a flitch would be so hard that it would rapidly dull the super-sharp cutter knife, and so brittle that the veneer sheets may readily split, and so tough that its resistance could crack up the machine.

Slicing. The design of the slicer determines the method, but in general terms, the flitch is clamped horizontally to a moving carriage, called a plate or flitch table. The carriage moves up and down, bringing the flitch against the knife. In a shearing motion the knife slices veneer from the flitch at a preset thickness, 1/42, 1/40, 1/28, or 1/20. These are the modern thicknesses most commonly made. Veneer sheets flow like paper (3-5) down a gang of traveling belts to waiting operators who stack them with unfailing accuracy in exact order so that you can buy consecutive sheets for book matching. A new vacuum-type cutter (3-6) holds the heavy flitch solely by vacuum. It saves hours of setup time.

The slicing methods described apply to plain, flat-cut slicing, flat-cut quartered, and quar-

3-4. Cherry flitch in the clutches of a machine called "the dragon" is on its way to a hot bath

25

tered. Fresh-cut veneers must next go to mechanical driers to reduce moisture content. (3-7)

Rotary cutting. This is an entirely different type of operation. In this method the log is locked in a lathe and is revolved against a fixed-position knife which peels veneer from the log. Theoretically it could unpeel the entire log at a rate of 200 to 400 feet per minute. The rotary-cut system produces the widest sheets of any method. (3-8) Some mills cut a groove the length of the log before it is mounted in the lathe. This groove acts as an automatic cutoff as the sheets are peeled from the log. It eliminates the danger of having the sheet tear before it reaches a chopping blade.

Saw cutting. The method of saw cutting started centuries ago. Even into this century it remained the standard method of producing veneers. Now it is little used. For one thing it is much too wasteful of prime woods, because the wide saw kerf turns to sawdust.

Half-round cutting. This system is similar to rotary cutting. Here, however, only half a log goes into the lathe at a time. The half-round log

3-5. Veneer slicer. Flitch, fastened to plate, moves down into cutter. Veneer sheets flow out like paper to waiting operators who stack them in consecutive order

is pinioned in the lathe off center so that as it rotates it comes into contact with the knife only on a half-rotation cycle. Burls, butts, and crotches are frequently cut in this manner.

How to cut a log is determined by veneer plant experts on the basis of market demand and their judgment for getting the best value from the log. Each of the cutting methods described produces a markedly different figuration. To visualize the wide variety of cutting options available, study the accompanying diagrams which show standard ways to cut a log.

The tree diagram (3-9) shows how one of the largest cherry veneer manufacturers delegates the parts of a tree trunk which will be cut into veneer. Cross-section diagrams (3-10) show broken lines to indicate the direction of the cut for flat-cut, flat-cut quartered, quartered, and half-round methods. Each direction of cut produces its own charcteristic figure which you will learn to recognize by examining the diagrams and wood-grain photographs to follow.

3-6. This is a new type of slicer. Heavy flitch, still hot and water-soaked from bath, is held against carriage screen solely by vacuum. Screen moves up and down. Slicer knife at left

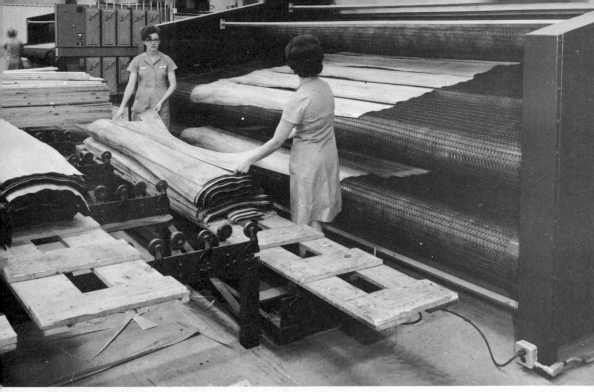

3-7. Veneer sheets from the slicer are fed into jet driers where moisture content is reduced

3-8. Rotary cutting produces widest sheets of veneer, theoretically endless as the log rotates in a lathe against a fixed cutter. (Below)

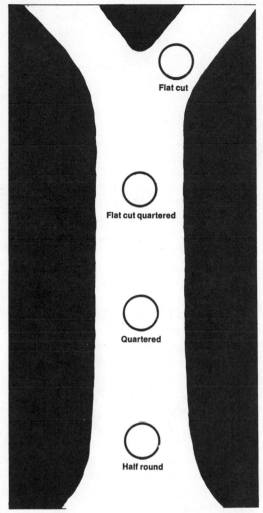

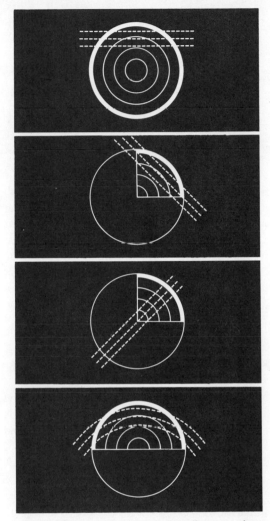

Flat cut

Flat cut quartered

Quartered

Half round

3-9. Tree diagram shows areas of cherry logs delegated to different cutting techniques at the veneer plant. This is typical procedure, but in practice each log presents its own special problem because of diameter, length or twist

3-10. Broken lines in cross-section diagrams show direction of cutter knife entering log.

Flat-cut method. Log is cut into roughly squared flitch or half flitch. Cherry is cut in half-flitches which are mounted so that they move up and down against the knife.

Flat-cut quartered. Log is sawed into quarters and cut parallel to growth rings.

Quartered. Quartered log contacts the blade at right angles to the growth rings.

Half-round. Log is cut into halves and mounted in lathe so that it revolves against knife and is sliced across the growth rings. This method creates a grainier, leafier figure

4. Kinds of veneers you work with

Veneers are not easily assigned to categories, but veneer manufacturers call the interesting veneers face veneers. When you see this classification used you know that it indicates the most colorful and best figured kinds. As the term implies, face veneers are intended for whatever faces out and is seen. For exterior surfaces of furniture, cabinets, paneling, and craftwork you want face veneers because they enhance the appearance of your woodwork.

With only two or three exceptions, the veneers in the Partial List later in this chapter can be utilized successfully as face veneers.

Sizes. The veneers you buy will generally be available in a standard length of 36 inches. A few are sold in 8-foot lengths. Burls, butts, and crotches are not in standard sizes. Some kinds of face veneers are only 5 inches wide. Many kinds are sold 12 inches wide, but the natural size of the tree obviously determines the size of the available veneer. Veneers are sold by the square foot, but this does not mean that they will come to you a foot wide.

Until recent years, face veneers were likely to be 1/28 thick. Improved cutting methods are now making it possible to cut veneers much thinner. Face veneers are likely to be 1/42, 1/40, 1/28, or 1/20. Of course these thinner cuts provide more yardage from a valuable hardwood log and put more of the choice veneers on the market. While thinner veneers are apt to be more brittle, and to split more readily, they give you an advantage you will come to appreciate. The thinner a veneer, the less likely it is to warp.

Crossband. Veneers not generally classed as face veneers are called crossband. Poplar, sycamore, and plain mahogany are frequently selected for use as crossband. This term refers to the sheet of veneer used as part of the core of a panel you are preparing to veneer. (4-1) Poplar is almost universally the first choice as crossband. Poplar now comes 1/28 and 1/8. Some is flatcut, some rotary-cut. Widths range from about 8 inches up to 12 and sometimes wider.

It would be a mistake to think of sycamore and plain mahogany only as crossband. Both are desirable as back veneers. Mahogany, in fact, is about as elegant a back veneer as you could want. Some sheets of sycamore, with its delicate swirling figuration and its faint pinkish tinge, are quite attractive where a face veneer without conspicuous figure is desired.

You will sometimes read of a third veneer classification, plain, unfigured. What is generally meant by the term is a veneer of uninteresting color and grain, good for a back veneer but not attractive enough for use as a face veneer. It is a confusing term that refers to no particular kind of wood.

Color and figure. When you are selecting veneer you think in terms of the color you want and the figure you believe is appropriate to the

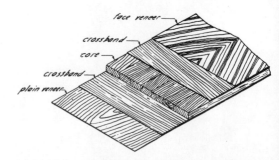

4-1. Crossband laid at right angle beneath exotic veneers like crotches and burls greatly reduces their natural tendency to twist, split, or blister

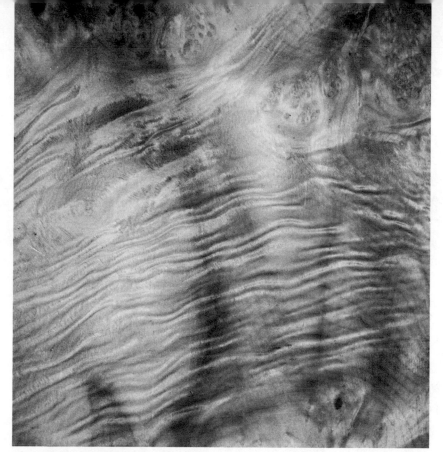

4-9. Myrtle swirl pattern, dominating area photographed, often runs into burl figure. Common also in poplar

intended use. The color range of some species is likely to vary remarkably. Flat-cut maple usually is white; bird's-eye maple is creamier with a faint reddish overtone; maple burl is creamy to reddish brown. Walnut is somewhat more uniform in color, greyish brown to darker brown, sometimes with a suggestion of purplish brown. Color, then, is not a completely reliable guide to identification; yet it is one of the best clues because it is far more uniform within a species than your next consideration, figure.

Figure within a species can range from straight stripes to curls, circles, waves, and waterfalls. Two factors influence the distinctive figure in the veneer you select. First, the actual physical structure of the wood will vary within the same species. Secondly, the way the log is cut has a critical influence on figure. Angle of cut has the greatest influence.

Diagrams in the previous chapter illustrated the conventional cutting methods now in use in veneer manufacturing plants. The results of these various methods can now be seen by examining the closeup photographs of wood grain. To keep the demonstration in the family only one species of wood will be used. It will be walnut, because this is one of the woods that comes in markedly different and beautiful varieties. Not all species produce the six types of wood grain shown for walnut. In fact no single walnut tree is likely to produce all six kinds in marketable quantities. The diagram of the walnut tree (4-2) indicates the general areas of a tree which yield particular figures.

There are numerous descriptive names such as bee's-wing, fiddleback, rope, curly, mottle, peanut, leaf, flake, and quilted which are applied to veneer figures. They are somewhat helpful terms, but cannot always be relied upon. Mottle, for example, has wide variation. It can appear

Rotary walnut ∧

4-3. Upper left, walnut crotch. 4-4. Lower left, typical striped pattern of quartered walnut. 4-5. Below, walnut butt. Walnut is most available butt figure. Only four species produce butt. 4-7. Above, walnut cut by rotary slicing, used for plywood

Crotch walnut ∧　　**∨ Quartered walnut**　　　　　　　　　　　**∨ Butt walnut**

4-2. Diagram below indicates general areas of tree which yield particular figure. 4-6. Right, close-up photo of walnut burl figure. 4-8. Lower right, typical figuration when walnut is flat-cut sliced

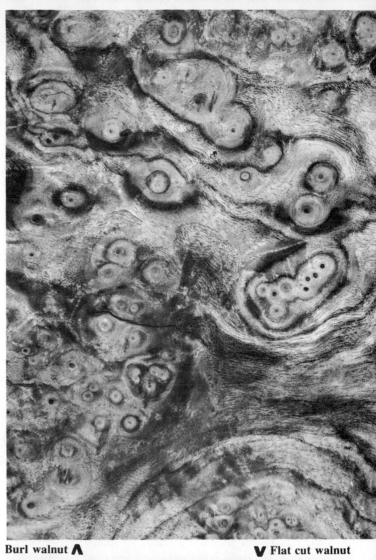

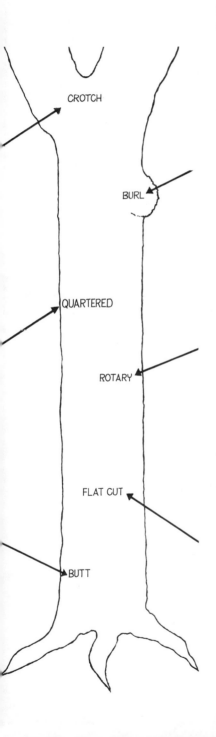

CROTCH

BURL

QUARTERED

ROTARY

FLAT CUT

BUTT

Burl walnut ∧   **∨ Flat cut walnut**

barely detectable in a small area, or prominently repeated over a sizable sheet of veneer. The mottle in satinwood is usually a lot more pronounced than the mottle in mahogany, but the opposite can also be found. One piece of mahogany can have more mottle than one piece of satinwood. What is called blistered by one person may be called quilted or curly by another. The terms are helpful but not precise.

Butts and burls, crotches and swirls

There are, however, four universal exotic figures with reliable names: butts, burls, crotches, and swirls. Although the character of walnut burl looks nothing like the character of poplar burl, there is no mistaking walnut burl from walnut crotch. They are as different as two woods can be. One slight exception should be mentioned. Swirl figure may run into crotch and burl. This mix is shown in a wood-grain photograph of myrtle. (4-9) Confluence of swirl and burl is commonly found in poplar and myrtle.

Crotch (4-3) comes from the area just below the fork in the tree trunk or where large branches join the trunk. At these points the fibers of the wood have been crushed and twisted between the forking branches. Tree sections from these areas may be cut into crotch veneer by either of two cutting methods, flat-cut or half-round.

Veneers cut from the crotch area sometimes acquire fancy names like horsetail, ponytail, feather, flame, and moon. Veneer experts say that crotch veneer should always be illustrated upside down to its growth, and that when used vertically, crotch veneer should be positioned in the same manner, as shown here in the crotch walnut photograph. (4-3)

Butt. (4-5) Another name for butt figure is stumpwood which is often used because it more clearly defines the location of tree area from which butt veneer is cut. At the junction of largest roots with the trunk of the tree the fibers are considerably distorted. They are twisted by a change from lateral to vertical direction and compressed by the tremendous weight of the entire tree.

Butt veneer is cut in commercial quantities from very few species of trees and, in fact, from very few trees, but when cut it has a distinctive character that is unlike any other veneer cut from the tree. Cutting butt sections from the tree is difficult for loggers, and the cumbersome clumps are hard to manage at the mill. The normal cutting method for butt veneer is half-round.

Burls. (4-6) If the pattern of burls can be defined at all, it might be called a design made of repeated circles, and circles within circles, and eyes within tiny circles. It can be easily recognized because it is unlike any other natural design in wood. Furthermore, the burl design of each species is distinct and unlike the burl design of another species. Burl walnut is more intricate than other burls. It has numerous eyes, some of which are inclined to become loose. It is quite brittle. To offset the brittle nature of such burls as walnut, the veneer manufacturer may not dry the burl veneer as much as other veneer cuts. The higher moisture content left in burls tends to reduce brittleness and make them easier to handle safely. It should be pointed out that damaged burls, especially small holes where eyes have loosened and dropped out, can be quite easily repaired. Broken areas can be replaced without becoming conspicuous because the busy design of the burl can be utilized to hide joint lines.

Because of brittleness walnut burl is available in smaller pieces than most other burls such as the elegant Carpathian elm burl, for example, which has a tighter composition.

Burls are wart-like growths on the side of a tree trunk caused by some early injury to the tree. Burls contain dark piths of a large number of buds which have failed to develop into twigs and branches. Throughout the burl veneer, the fibers are irregularly contorted so that the grain cannot be said to run in any particular direction, but in virtually all directions. Burl veneer is exceptionally prized because nothing else is like it and it is manufactured in small quantities, necessarily limited to the infrequent burls on trees.

Swirls (4-10) This is a pattern of wavy lines. The illustrated example is mahogany swirl. No sample of walnut swirl could be located for photography. It is seldom possible to buy a sheet of veneer limited to swirl pattern. To some degree this shortage is caused by manufacturers who cannot readily separate the swirl pattern from the crotch pattern because they merge. Swirl grows in front of and behind the area where crotch grows. There is no definite dividing line

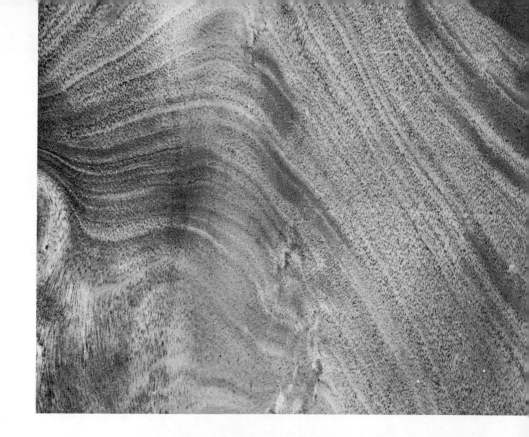

4-10. Swirl figure occurs in trees both in front of and behind crotch figure. Very few species produce swirl at all. Mahogany swirl, above, is a beautiful example. Notice its resemblance to crotch. Photograph at right shows poplar swirl, pale green with tan figure

4-11. A few samples from standard kit show one of best ways to learn color and figure of veneers used most in panel veneering and craftwork. All samples show name and where found

between crotches and swirls. One gradually changes into the other. Crotches are highly desired choice veneer cuts and are favored when the log section is prepared for cutting.

Quartered walnut. (4-4) The cross-section cutting diagram in chapter 3 showed two ways to slice a log after it has been cut into quarters. The difference in the direction a knife blade enters the log makes considerable difference in figure. The flat-cut quartered method produces a leafier, heart pattern. The conventional quartered method produces a striped pattern which is what most people think of when they want quarter-cut veneer. The wood-grain photograph of quartered walnut (4-4) is typical of quarter-cutting. The figure is striped.

Rotary-cut walnut. (4-7) Rotary cutting has been practiced as long as veneers have been cut by machine, but rotary cutting does not make the best use of a valuable log like walnut. Consequently walnut is rotary cut only for panel manufacturers who want wide sheets that demand little or no joining. It rarely reaches the crafts-

man market. Rotary cutting produces a wild, leafy, irregular figure not in a class with veneers cut by other methods.

A few woods lend themselves better to rotary cutting and are still being cut by this method. Bird's-eye maple is one. Poplar crossband is another. Many hardwoods are cut by the rotary method for panel manufacturers, but 95% of the veneers you will use have been sliced.

Flat-cut walnut. (4-8) The pattern produced by flat cutting is characterized by a combination of straight grain and heart figure. The keynote is the heart figure, usually a long, irregular oval or series of such ovals one within the next. This design is the feature that distinguishes flat-cut veneer from the more uniformly striped quarter-cut veneer. For flat cutting, the log is cut into halves which are mounted in turn on the slicer. The slicer knife cuts straight through the heart of the half section.

Not all wood species are cut into each of the figures that have been detailed. Of the four exotic types of figure described—butts, burls, crotches, and swirls—the craftsman cannot count on locating more than a few kinds of wood showing these unusual and highly prized patterns. Only a few species produce the desired logs, and not always in commercial quantities sufficient to make production worthwhile or economically practical. The wood suppliers listings are the best sources for finding which kinds of the exotic veneers are offered.

Clues to identification. Craftsmen who have explored the science of wood technology know that many clues must be examined before a particular wood specimen can be identified. The rest of us who work with prized veneers because they make our woodworking projects more beautiful are generally content to develop a keen sense of wood identification without becoming involved with the microscope.

The descriptions and wood-grain photographs of walnut serve well as an introduction to identification. The figuration characteristics of walnut are typical of many other woods. No two species and no two sheets of veneer come out just alike, but you can use the illustrated examples as clues to be applied in general to other woods. In other words, crotch pattern of other woods will

follow the walnut crotch sufficiently for identifying the pattern; quarter cuts show a striped pattern; flat-cuts have a heart pattern; rotary displays a wild, undisciplined pattern. These clues are helpful as a beginning to identification.

About 60 woods you should know appear in a forthcoming list. Very brief descriptions of color and figure provide additional clues. A good study method would be to refer to the list while you examine the wood-grain photographs presented throughout this book.

Wood samples. The veneers themselves are the ultimate source for clues. Samples of many of the world's choice veneers have been assembled in convenient sample kits. Each square of veneer measures 4x9 and is labeled for ready identification. The veneers in these kits provide the best source for study and are large enough for many craftwork projects and pictures. One of the standard sample kits offered by wood suppliers is illustrated. (4-11)

In repair work on fine furniture, wood samples are almost essential. Among the 50 samples in one kit you can ordinarily locate a near-match to replace a small damaged area on a table, chest, desk, antique clock, or cabinet.

Partial list of veneers most often used by craftsmen

Amboyna (East Indies) rich brown variegated yellow to red. Burls.

Ash (USA) cream colored with brown, open stripes.

Aspen (USA) white to whitish yellow with light brown markings. Varieties: straight stripe, mottle, crotch.

Avodire (Africa) whitish yellow to pale yellow gold. Faint wavy design from reflected light comes and goes. Varieties: plain, stripe, mottle.

Beech (USA) predominately white, some with pale reddish brown flecks somewhat resembling lacewood.

Benge (Africa) light brown with dark brown and red-brown stripes.

Benin (Africa) also called benin walnut. Grey brown to gold with black streaks. Crotches sometimes available.

Birch (USA) tan with light brown faint wavy grain.

Bubinga (Africa) pinkish red with wavy lines of purple.

Butternut (USA) pale brown, leafy grain converging into superimposed cathedral patterns resembling oak, but actually related to walnut.

Carpathian elm burl (England and France) brick red to light tan. Attractive pattern of circles and central eyes.

Cherry (Africa) *see* Makori.

Cherry (USA) light reddish brown. Open wavy pattern, usually not pronounced.

Ebony, Gaboon (Africa) black. Very little visible figure. Hard to cut.

Ebony, Macassar (East Indies) dark brown to black, streaked faintly with yellow. Tough to cut.

Eucalyptus (Australia) tan to gold, sometimes with flashes of pink. Blistered, ripple and fiddleback figures.

Faux satine (USA) related to cypress. Yellowish brown, straight stripe. Soft.

Goncalo alves (Brazil) dark brown with straight tan streaks.

Gumwood (USA) reddish brown and tan usually highly patterned. Easy to work.

Harewood (England) sycamore dyed silver grey. Beautiful color. Faint figure, lightly striped. Some has a faint fiddleback reflection.

Holly (USA) white, turning light brown with age. Soft. Used for inlay contrast.

Kelobra (Mexico) brown with greenish cast. Streaked or large pattern of wavy lines.

Koa (Hawaii) golden brown with dark brown streaks and sometimes wavy. Often fiddleback.

Lacewood (Australia) light pinkish coloration. Flecked prominently with brown. Flecks range from tiny to 1/8 inch or more.

Lauan (Philippines) formerly known as Philippine mahogany. Pale pinkish color, very faint straight markings. Used mainly by manufacturers of plywood and hollow-core doors.

Limba (Africa) also known as Korina. Pale yellow to light brown.

Madrone burl (USA) reddish brown, sometimes pinkish.

Mahogany. Many kinds. African is light pink to reddish brown and sometimes tannish brown. Honduras is light reddish to yellowish brown, also dark red. Mahogany figures vary from plain, faintly striped to beautiful mottled patterns and extraordinary crotches.

Makori (Africa) also called African cherry. Pinkish brown to reddish brown. Has varying degrees of ripple crossfire and interesting sheen. One of the most handsome dark veneers.

New Guinea wood (New Guinea) yellow with dark brown irregular stripes.

Oak (England) darker brown than American varieties. Close markings of dark brown, slightly wavy.

Oak (USA) tan with broad arrow markings of brown grain, or with light tan rift, cross ripples.

Orientalwood (Australia) greyish brown, straight stripes. Occasionally with pinkish cast. Dark tone.

Padauk (Andaman Islands and Burma) golden brown and close red stripes, usually with a violet-red tinge.

Paldao (Philippines) grey to reddish brown in irregular striped pattern, somewhat wild.

Pecan (USA) reddish brown with dark streaks. Prominent, irregular pattern.

Poplar (USA) Crossband, pale yellow. Greenish, brownish streaks. Mostly straight striped, usually somewhat angular striping because most poplar veneer is rotary cut.

Primavera (Central America) very pale yellow, sometimes nearly white, sometimes yellowish brown. Faint figure in a succession of closely woven, quite wavy stripes. Primavera mottle has a changing sheen that moves with light reflection.

Purpleheart (Central America, South America, and Dutch Guiana) actually turns purple as it ages. Color varies from medium purple to dark purple. Grain is faint, striped, uninteresting, but the color is fascinating.

Redwood burl (USA) reddish brown to deep red. Closely packed burls, or eyes. A handsome veneer, but tends to crumble at cut edges unless handled with extra care.

Rosewood. There are three available veneer varieties. Brazilian is characterized by combinations of tan, light golden brown, and dark brown mixes with streaks of very dark brown, almost black. Pattern is striped and wavy. East Indian rosewood is dark purple to ebony with streaks of red or yellow. Pattern is straight striped. Honduras rosewood is lighter than Brazilian. Is likely to have a somewhat orange-brown coloring mixed with dark brown. Pattern is irregular striped, not as wavy as Brazilian.

Sapele (Africa) dark reddish brown. Has a visible but not prominent straight-striped pattern with little variation in color of stripes. Crossfire flecks make the veneer sparkle. Easy to work.

Satinwood (Ceylon) pale gold to deeper yellow-gold. Has several characteristic figure patterns: straight and somewhat wavy, or rippled, faint stripes; mottle; and bee's-wing mottle. One of the world's most elegant veneers.

Sycamore (USA) pale tan, almost white, with very faint pinkish grain in irregular stripes and broad swirls.

Tamo (Japan) tan with wild and wavy brown grain ranging from leaf pattern to narrow wavy stripes and a prominent small pattern called peanut shell, and resembling its name.

Teak (Burma) yellowish light brown with darker brown streaks. Figure varies from plain stripes to mottle and somewhat leafy pattern created by medium brown streaks.

Thuya burl (Africa) golden brown to reddish brown with dark brown eyes. Pattern twists and swirls around numerous eyes.

Tulipwood (Brazil) light background of yellowish tan streaked with red and purple. Leafy, wavy, and irregular stripes intermixed.

Walnut, claro (USA) tannish brown with dark brown. Prominent wavy stripes, sometimes in a repeating design of scallops.

Walnut, French (France) greyish brown, lighter and more brownish than American walnut. More prominently grained than flat-cut and quarter-cut American black walnut.

Walnut (USA) light grey-brown, actually more grey than brown. Wide range of figures: plain striped, leafy pattern, also butts, burls, and crotches.

Zebrano or **Zebrawood** (Africa) straw color with either straight or slightly wavy dark brown stripes. Brittle, but workable with extra care when cutting and handling.

Super-thin flexible veneer. In the past there have been attempts to produce large sheets of real-wood veneer with flexible backing. Until recently most products of that type were not completely successful. Now, however, wood suppliers offer the craftsman a broad choice of excellent super-thin flexible veneer sheets that perform well in all respects. (4-12) These sheets, only 1/64 thick, come 8 feet long in widths of 18, 24, and 36. The sheets resist tearing and splitting. They tolerate bending so well that they can be applied satisfactorily to curved surfaces and can be manipulated safely when being applied to large flat surfaces.

What this advance means to the craftsman is that projects once considered impractical are now being accomplished with reasonable ease. For example, you can now apply veneer, as a restoration technique, without bending forms or cauls, to the curved door of a cabinet or to the serpentine drawer front of a chest. You can re-surface coffee tables, dining tables, interior doors, desks, chests, headboards, and many other large areas with a single sheet of veneer. The uncertainties of accurate jointing large sheets are eliminated. In combination with

4-12. Super-thin, flexible veneer comes in rolls. Tolerates bending, handling, large or curved work

instant-set contact glue, the thin sheets of veneer open up new areas of decorative upgrading in the home woodworking shop.

Flexible veneer is available in a substantial variety of woods: cherry, maple, teak, walnut, mahogany, rosewood, oak, and birch.

Benin crotch

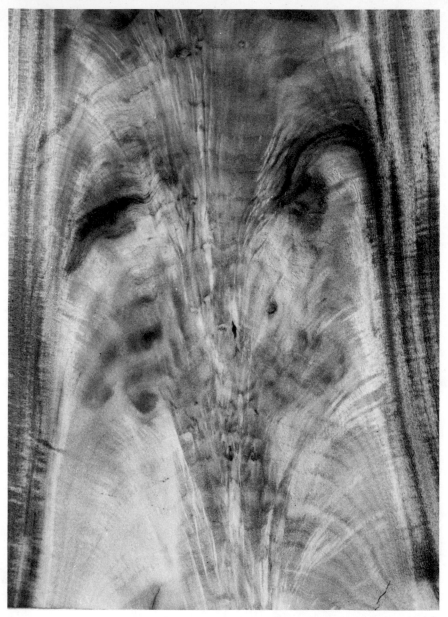

Aspen crotch

DYED VENEERS

Selection. Most dyed veneers available in America are imported from France or Italy. Most, but not all, of the 1/28 dyed veneers have no figure, or it is so faint that the figure is not noticeable. The woods best suited to dyeing are sycamore, birch, maple, aspen, and a few others. Only sycamore has sufficient figure pattern to show up appreciably after dyeing.

A thinner variety, and considerably more brittle, is now coming in from Europe. It has more figure, usually straight stripe composed of hard grain in strong color and soft grain in subdued color. This characteristic creates a striped effect that is more interesting than the plainer 1/28 dyed veneers. The dyed kinds require more careful handling. The author has successfully cut intricate designs from this thinner variety with a

Aspen mottle ⋀

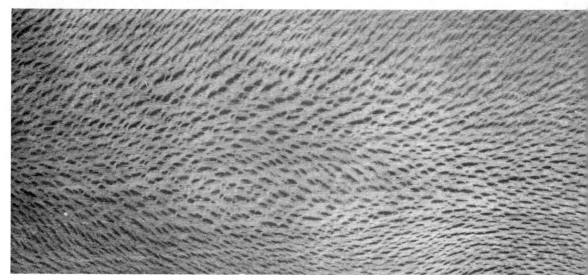

Sycamore, flake figure ⋀   ⋁ Lacewood, flake figure

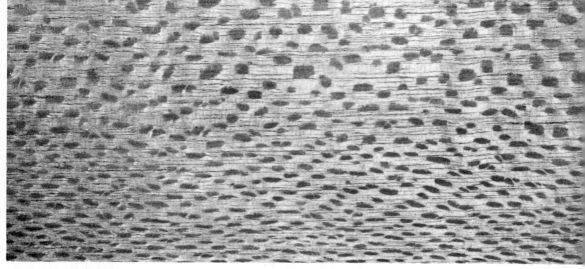

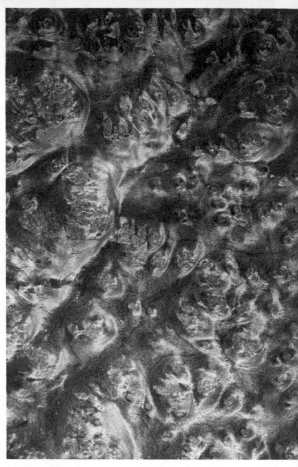

Carpathian elm burl

Madrone burl

Olive ash burl

Maple burl

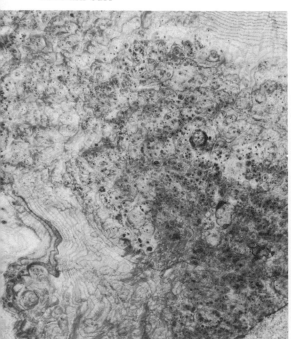

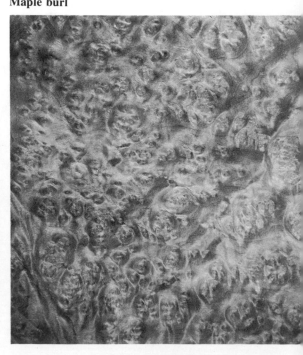

Redwood burl

Myrtle burl

Avodire mottle ∧

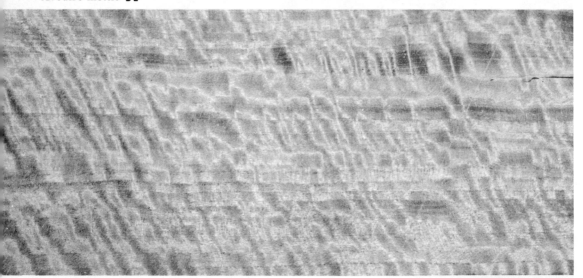

Satinwood mottle ∧   **∨ Peroba mottle**

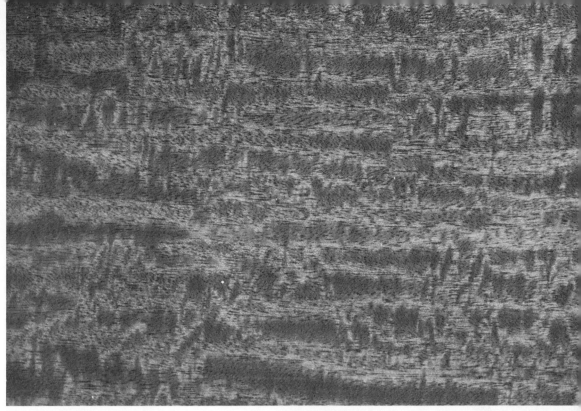

Mahogany mottle

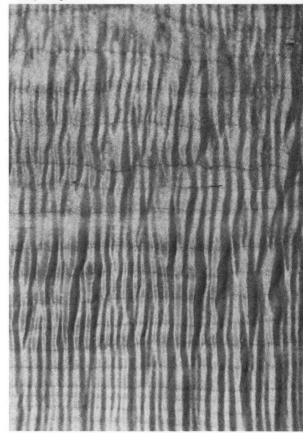

Curly maple

craft knife, just to demonstrate that it can be worked when special care is exercised in handling and cutting. Suggested cutting techniques are detailed in the section on cutting veneers, chapter 7.

Colors. You could name a color you want and could probably find a dyed veneer coming close to your request. This partial list indicates the wide variety: sunset red, mahogany red, flamingo pink, tropic green, Gulf Stream green, purple, yellow, midnight blue, black, and a stunning white made of bird's-eye maple.

Appropriate uses. Most craftsmen prefer to find a natural veneer to add color value to their work. However, when natural veneers are not brilliant enough for the purpose, they introduce dyed veneers in small areas. Common uses in marquetry include birds, flowers, clothing, brickwork, sunsets, and so on. There is no question that dyed woods add a bright and lively decorative feature to craftwork.

5. Tools, equipment, and suggested uses

Cutting tools and accessories. The two most important cutting tools are veneer saw and craft knife. (5-1) They are essential for getting out work-size sheets of veneer. The saw is better than the knife for this purpose. Before invention of the veneer saw, the dovetail saw was used for straight cuts, and some craftsmen still use it on veneer. The best knife for cutting veneer is craft knife No. 1-C with the sharp-pointed, tapered No. 11 blade.

A used hacksaw blade with teeth filed down for protection of fingers and veneer makes an ideal short straightedge. When a longer straightedge is required, use the 24-inch steel square. A single-edge razor blade cuts veneer very fast and clean. Veneer handlers use it freehand, without measure or straightedge, to cut off a work piece from a large sheet.

A handy edging tool for reducing irregular overhang prior to sanding is the tiny trimming plane, only 3½ inches long. For edge jointing your equipment should include something

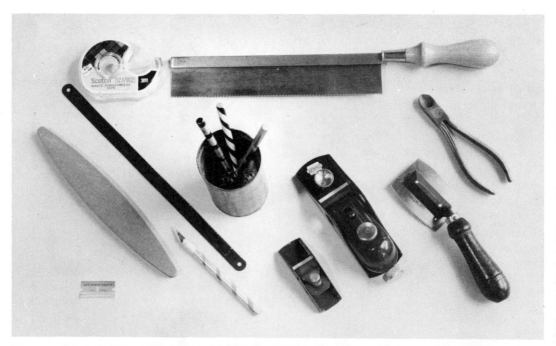

5-1. Assortment of cutting tools and aids. Veneer saw, bottom right, and craft knife cut veneer best. Planes are for trimming and jointing edges. Old hacksaw blade makes handiest 12-inch straightedge to own. Knife pot with cushioned filler keeps knives handy, fingers safe. Clear gum tape reduces splits from knife-cutting

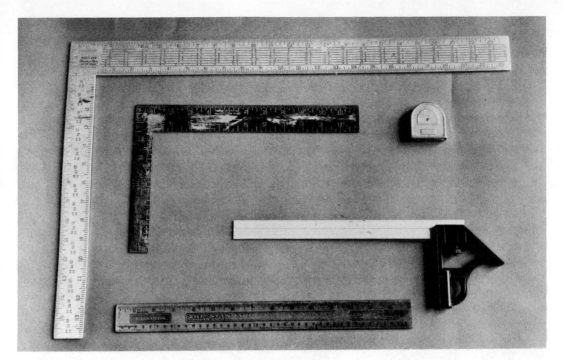

5-2. Measuring tools. Steel squares make the most accurate layouts on veneers and panels. They also serve as rules and straightedges. The 24-inch size, often essential, is cumbersome to use on small work. Smaller square is handier, quicker. Combination square is useful on panel layouts where head can overhang an edge.

larger, a standard block plane or a smoothing plane. When you drive veneer pins to tighten a joint temporarily while gum tape is drying, you can leave the pins projecting, but in some other uses you will want to cut off the pins. Sharp nippers do the closest job. Clear gum tape and a sharpening stone round out the cutting accessories.

Measuring tools. You can get along easily with less variety in tools for measuring, but the assortment illustrated (5-2) adds convenience and often saves work time. Both steel squares, 24-inch and 12-inch, serve as layout tools and as straightedges for saw and knife cutting. The 12-inch combination square is useful for testing squareness of small squares of veneer, and the 24-inch square can be used for testing squareness of larger sheets. In addition, the tool assortment includes a handier measuring instrument, the common rule. This one is 15 inches, far more practical than a 12-inch rule. Since the custom-

ary size of veneer sheets is 36 inches, the 6-foot rule is essential.

Cleanup tools. An emery board gets into small spaces that are too cramped or too dangerous for the sanding block. If your work requires other shapes of sanding sticks, wrap very fine sandpaper or 150-C garnet around several diameters of dowels, halfround molding, and flat sticks. (5-3)

After sanding, clean up with a small brush. Use it also to sweep your workboard free of sanding grit and veneer shards that could scratch work sheets of veneer. The most appropriate tool for safe removal of stubborn gum paper from veneer faces is the old-time cabinet scraper, or hand scraper, for which a handled cabinet scraper now popular is a dangerous substitute unless corners are dulled. The square chisel and chisel blade in the craft-knife holder are essential for scraping off the hardened glue and filler applied to obscure joints and splits.

5-3. Cleanup tools. Craft knife, fitted with small scraper blade, and straight chisel are used for cleaning glue squeeze-out and filled joints. Cabinet scraper removes gum paper from laid veneer faces. Brush cleans sanding dust from wood pores. Emery board and sanding block smooth edges

Workboards. You need several sizes of workboards, depending upon your type of work. Most craftsmen like a couple of small boards in the range of 12 x 15 and larger boards about 24 square. If you cut a lot of full sheets their full length, you can get by without a larger board but it means moving the veneer to continue cutting its full length. To avoid this doubtful practice, have available a workboard 18 x 38. Use it as a super top to protect your worktable all of the time. These boards all serve as gluing cauls.

That means you need several in matching sizes.

Fir plywood is not satisfactory. It is too bumpy. The best choice is semi-soft, but firm, flakeboard, also known as particle board. Nearly all lumberyards now have a variety of cutoffs. The most convenient is ⅜ but ½ will serve. Avoid ¾ because it is needlessly heavy to handle. When your workboard becomes too scarred from saw and knife, turn it over. After that, use it as a core panel. Scratches improve the glue bond.

6. Modern glues and easier gluing methods

Every woodworker of long experience is likely to have acquired a strong preference for a particular brand of glue. He has probably used a lot of it with acceptable success. Gluing veneer, however, is not like gluing mortise-and-tenon joints or other members of solid construction. New factors must be allowed for. Glues for veneering must have special qualities. Hot glue is a poor choice for veneering, now that fast-setting, stain-free glues have been developed.

The three types of adhesives illustrated (6-1) have been used for projects throughout this book. They adapt themselves to veneering. Each type fulfills a special requirement. The brands illustrated are not claimed to be necessarily superior to other brands of similar type.

6-1. Glues for craftwork and panel veneering as demonstrated throughout this book must be fast, strong, and non-staining. Three modern ready-mixed glues met all requirements described

Modern glues have revolutionized veneering methods. The glue pot for melting hide flakes has graduated into the hands of the antiques dealer. Chemical glues have entered the woodworking shop. They are cleaner, faster, stronger, and they dry without a conspicuous glue line. Industrial chemists have developed an overwhelming array of specialty adhesives for every imaginable industrial requirement. Fortunately for the veneer craftsman only a few demand consideration. The three that have been chosen for veneering demonstrations in this book represent the simplified approach to modern veneering. They meet the normal requirements of the average veneer craftsman.

One conspicuous advantage these modern glues possess is that they are ready-mixed. After the glue pot bowed out, the scales and spoons for weighing and measuring the powders and catalysts came into the shop. Mixing by guess was even more common. Today you can glue small panels, both flat and curved, and accomplish all craftwork without the nuisance, lost time, and uncertainties of mixing.

There is still another reason for choosing no-mix glues whenever possible. They have a long shelf life; that is, they are ready when the work is ready. Glues requiring mixing have a usable life of only a few hours at most. A person doing craftwork may need a small amount of glue every hour or two as work progresses. Stopping work to mix more glue is an unnecessary aggravation.

What qualities other than ready-mixed should be considered when you select the appropriate glue for the veneering project being undertaken?

It is an over-simplification to put the three types into size categories; yet, as a first but not final consideration, each type because of special qualities is adapted to size of project.

In terms of size, small projects favor white glue. Medium projects favor yellow glue (Titebond.) Large projects favor contact veneer glue.

The next considerations are more specific; that is, technical questions must be answered when choosing the right glue for a particular project.

Is it fast enough? Will it set in a few minutes? A few hours? Days? Will it set fast enough to permit work on the project to progress while you have available time?

Is it too fast for assembly? Does it set faster than you can spread and equalize glue coverage on the entire mounting surface?

Is it strong enough for the assignment? Will it resist the pull of veneer having a natural tendency to warp? Will it take hold of an oily veneer and prevent it from blistering?

Can temperature requirements be met where the gluing will be handled?

How much weighting or clamping is required? Is the necessary clamping equipment on hand? Should a different glue be used to fit the clamping equipment?

Will it leave a dark glue line in a conspicuous area?

Can squeeze-out be cleaned off without unsightly discoloration?

Will it respond to the simple technique for applying heat for resetting a blister? Chapter 14 shows this simple and important technique.

Will it set so hard and set so fast that you must have a helper?

The following brief summaries relating to product characteristics have come partly from product bulletins of glue manufacturers. Recommendations and conclusions come from the author's experience while using all three types of glue for veneering projects.

White glue, polyvinyl resin

This type is recognized by everyone. The brand illustrated is Elmer's Glue-All. Some other brands of synthetic resin glues known as polyvinyl acetate and polyvinyl resin are also suitable. For simplicity this group will be called white glue.

White glue is fast setting but not too fast for assembly. After applying, wait 3 minutes before assembly. Maximum waiting time, during assembly, is 10 minutes. Temperature of room and wood should be about 70 degrees.

One of the major advantages of white glue is its relative delayed set. It allows time for laying more than one piece of veneer on a panel. For instance, if you are applying back veneer in two pieces because a single piece was not available, you have time to glue one piece, lay it on the panel and weight it temporarily while you lay the

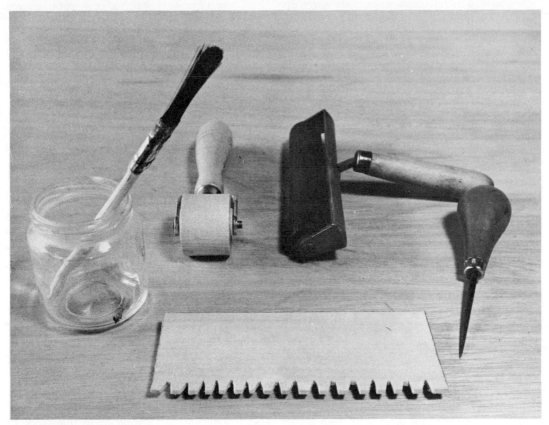

6-2. Homemade wooden glue comb spreads glue fast. Brushes move glue to edges and make coat even. Awl holds veneer down when brushing. Rollers assure complete contact of veneer to panel

second piece beside the first. Then you still have time to draw the pieces together to create a good joint.

White glue containers specify short clamping time. In veneering you should allow hardwoods to remain in clamps or under weights for a minimum of 40 minutes. To be on the safe side leave glue-ups for several hours or even overnight. Don't trim overhang of a panel for at least 12 hours.

White glue leaves almost no visible glue line. Smeared glue on light veneers leaves a slight discoloration.

Brushes and glue spreaders are easily cleaned with warm water if cleaned at once. Brushes that are moistened before use are easier to clean.

Blisters caused by poor contact can be heated and pressed back into place.

Small craftwork can be safely weighted instead of clamped when you use white glue, unless the veneer is especially unruly. You take a little more risk weighting white glue than yellow.

If veneer gluing is new to you, the foregoing basic questions about glue selection should be reviewed, at least in the beginning until appropriate decisions become automatic.

Yellow glue, aliphatic emulsion

This is a ready-mixed glue of aliphatic type. The brand illustrated is Titebond. For simplicity it will be referred to here as yellow glue.

Yellow glue sets fast. It develops tack faster than white glue. It becomes stiffer and is harder to spread. It would be difficult to spread over a large area with hand methods. It allows slightly less assembly time than white glue.

51

Because of its early tack, or resistance, you do not have as much time as white glue allows for shifting members of an assembly to correct their relative positions. Any required adjustment must be made without delay.

Room temperatures for yellow glue can be 75 degrees or more, and this applies to veneer and panel as well. This is a fairly high working temperature, but it improves the spreading characteristic of yellow glue.

Coverage should be heavy and even.

You can determine whether you were within allowable assembly time on your first job by looking for edge squeeze-out. If glue bubbles do not appear at the edge when clamps are tightened, either you took too much assembly time or you spread less glue than required. Uniform clamping pressure is more important than very heavy pressure.

Minimum time in clamps or under weights is about 40 minutes. More setting time is recommended, up to 2 hours. Don't trim overhang for 12 hours. Soft glue bubbles at edges do not indicate soft glue inside the assembly.

Yellow glue leaves almost no visible glue line. A slight stain is noticed on light veneer surfaces. Squeeze-out is easiest to clean off if you work at it within one hour after clamping. You can reach most edges while the assembly is still in clamps.

Yellow glue makes a stronger bond. It is preferable for non-porous, dense woods and for non-porous panels such as hardboard. It is better also for assembling solid hardwood strips being used to build up a panel core.

Brushes and glue spreaders can be cleaned with warm water. Blisters can be heated and pressed down for better contact, providing there is glue under the blister.

Clamping and weighting requirements are about the same as for white glue. Yellow glue may possibly improve your chances over white glue when weights alone are used.

Instant-set contact adhesive

The third type of glue shown, veneer contact glue, is fast becoming first choice with veneer craftsmen because of its unique qualities. It sets on contact and thereby virtually eliminates an assortment of presses, clamps, and elaborate devices such as cauls and crossbearers.

This glue has a wait period of 40 to 60 minutes after spreading. An additional wait period of 30 to 60 minutes significantly increases bonding strength and is recommended. It should not be left for more than about 3 hours.

Porous surfaces, such as most veneers, should have a second coat, and the panel the same treatment, the second coat coming about 60 minutes after the first.

After assembly there is no required wait period. Clamping and weighting are recommended nevertheless for a short period.

Room and parts should be between 70 and 90 degrees.

Bond strength is very high. Glue line is virtually invisible.

Laying two glued surfaces together calls for a slipsheet and careful alignment. Large or complicated assemblies require a helper.

Brushes and spreaders while still wet can be partially cleaned with soapy water. Lacquer thinner finishes the cleanup.

Blisters can be heated and pressed down if there is glue on both surfaces under the blister.

Gluing aids

A few simple tools, cleaned up after the previous glue job, are a welcome convenience to have ready and within easy reach. (6-2)

Brushes are the best glue spreaders for areas up to about one square foot. Two sizes are enough for average work: ½-inch and 1-inch. Of course you should buy a 3-inch size if you customarily handle large glue jobs. When you glue panels of roughly chessboard size, brushes are too slow. For contact type glues, brushes with Nylon bristles are the best choice.

Comb. For large areas, or even smaller areas when fast-set glues are being used, you should make yourself a wooden comb glue spreader of scrap ¼-inch stock. Notch one edge, leaving square tips on the comb, not pointed tips which break off too easily. Anything fancier than the comb illustrated will not work any better. Be sure to make your glue comb of wood, not metal. Some of the modern glues react unfavorably to metal, especially to iron. The glue absorbs iron which then reacts on such woods as oak, walnut, and mahogany by forming a black glue line which you will not be able to remove.

The homemade glue spreader provides fast

coverage, but you will have to equalize coverage and carry glue to the edges with a brush.

Keep a glass jar at hand while you work. Drop the brush in there, handle down, when it is loaded with glue.

Rollers in two sizes are useful. A small wooden roller is ideal for veneered edges of panels. A large rubber roller is better for large areas. Never run the rubber roller across bare veneer; rubber can stain wood. Lay a sheet of wax paper between veneer and roller. Rolling pins sound great as rollers, but are not nearly as handy as one-hand rollers. Don't spare the rollers. Use them even when contact glue is the adhesive used.

Veneer hammer. This homemade tool is a standard instrument in the cabinet shops of European craftsmen. Because it is individually made, it appears in a fascinating variety of styles and shapes.

The veneer hammer illustrated (6-3) started when the long wooden handle of a discarded floor buffer was cut short. New buffers were priced out at less than two dollars, but it is even cheaper to make your own, and for this purpose you will find a working drawing in Tricks of the Trade.

The sheepskin buffing pad and the wooden platen were set aside. A brass plate was cut to fit the hammer head and drilled to take two bolts fitted with wing nuts. Brass could be ¼, $^3/_{16}$, or ⅛, whichever thickness is obtainable. The bottom edge and corners of the brass plate were filed smooth and rounded. While called a hammer, it actually is a pressure device to be described further along in this chapter.

Awl for holding work. The glue brush drags when you are spreading glue. This resistance pulls the veneer sheet into fresh glue on the newspaper. Hold an awl on the veneer, but don't press so hard that you make a hole. Veneer softened by glue is easily punctured. A good safety precaution is to dull the point of the awl you use for gluing. The second precaution is to have newspapers prearranged so that you can carefully lift and shift the veneer to fresh paper while you work. It prevents smears on the good side of veneer.

Tweezers will help you move freshly glued small pieces of veneer to a mounting panel with

6-3. Veneer hammer, a variation of the roller, is an oldtime cabinetmaker's favorite. This one was made from discarded floor buffer with brass plate added for rubbing down glued veneer

6-4. Smooth hardboard surface is knife-scored to provide better glue bond for the veneer

less imprint in the glue than your thumb would leave.

Gluing techniques

Glues you use in veneering are not gap-fillers. There are some woodworking glues that make up for loose joints. In veneering you are using glues that work best between two surfaces that are well fitted but somewhat porous. Porosity of veneer permits a good glue bond. Porosity of flakeboard makes a good glue bond. But hardboard, on the glazed side, is not porous enough. To improve the glue bond, scratch the hardboard surface with a knife held slightly at an angle so that you create a slight under-cut scratch on the surface. (6-4) Be careful not to cut deeply, especially at the edges.

Clean surfaces. Just before applying glue take the wise precaution of brushing panel and veneer surfaces. Comb and shake sanding grit from the brush you are going to use. Clean

surfaces are the first essential in successful veneer gluing.

Application. When you have a choice, always apply glue to the panel, never to the veneer itself. If you are building a panel of layered veneers you must, of course, apply glue to veneer. In this case apply it to the crossband, not to the underside of the face veneer or the inside of the back veneer.

Glue hardens by giving up its moisture. The process starts upon exposure to air. If you spread glue on veneer, some of the moisture immediately enters the veneer. Moisture causes warp. It is better to spread glue on the more stable panel which can withstand moisture better than veneer can. White glue is being spread on a flakeboard panel with a glue comb. (6-5) Notice that it is being worked away from the edge. Later a brush will be used to move glue out to the edge.

Coverage. Applying glue from a squeeze bottle is a clean, easy, and controllable method. Get as even a deposit as you can by moving the bottle over the area as you squeeze out a steady stream of glue. Don't be carried away with the fun of making fancy designs or initials. You will be wasting precious time. Hold back from the edges. Use brush or wooden spreader to get distribution as even as possible, but do it quickly without trying to get complete coverage at first. Take special precaution to brush outward at edges, never inward, or you will mess up the edges. Have one or two damp, not soaking wet, paper towels ready. Use towels to wipe up excess glue around edges. Avoid smearing it around. Smeared glue is harder to remove later than actual glue bubbles. Add more glue to areas not fully covered.

Coverage should be complete, even, somewhat heavy. Experience will tell you what complete coverage means. One way to judge, after the fact, is to watch for squeeze-out as clamps are applied. If there is no squeeze-out, you did not apply sufficient glue around edges. Don't minimize coverage at edges to avoid squeeze-out. If you do, you invite moisture penetration and veneer lifting.

Lay panel on veneer. In assembly, whenever it is practical to do so, always lay the glue-fresh panel on top of the flat, marked veneer sheet.

The veneer sheet you previously prepared for

6-5. Fast glue spreader, notched scrap wood, being used to spread glue on flakeboard panel preparatory to laying on butternut veneer

6-6. Glue-fresh flakeboard panel laid on guidelines drawn on butternut veneer. Method reduces chance of glue moisture warping veneer

the panel should have been cut oversize, with about ¼-inch margin at every edge to be trimmed off later. Before you spread glue on the panel, lay the dry panel in position on the underside of the veneer. Mark a pencil line on the veneer by following around the panel as a guide. When the panel has been spread with glue, it can be laid quickly on the veneer sheet in exact position. (6-6) This is a far better method than the reverse—trying to position, blind, an oversize veneer sheet on a wet panel.

Glue blankets. The illustrated assembly of flakeboard and a sheet of butternut face veneer (6-6) now should go into clamps. This is a safer procedure than attempting to glue the back veneer on the panel at the same time. Pressure should be applied as soon as possible. Cauls and clamps must be in readiness and within easy reach. Clamps should be open to the approximate requirement.

Two sheets of brown paper cut to required size must be ready for use as glue blankets. Brown paper is better than wax paper for this purpose. It absorbs squeeze-out better and it allows penetra-

tion of moisture. Wax paper is more likely to hold glue moisture in the veneer. Glue hardens by losing its moisture. Don't retard drying of the glue or do anything that keeps moisture in the veneer.

Cut-up grocery bags provide satisfactory glue blankets if large enough and if you cut away the seams. Seams are acceptable on the bare caul but intolerable against face veneer.

Roller and hammer. The critical moment in veneering is now. More veneer failures are man-made at this moment than at any other. Glue is still wet and has developed very little holding power at this time. Before you place the glued-up assembly in clamps, roller the veneer hard against the panel. Use the veneer hammer, too, especially on large panels. (6-7) Work it zigzag down the center of the panel first, then down one side and the other, working finally to the very edges of the panel. This pressure you are applying with roller and hammer is forcing veneer against panel.

At this moment the veneer is getting wet from moisture in the glue. Moisture encourages veneer to buckle. You are offsetting the buckle with pressure and you are moving excess glue out to the glue line. Be reminded that the device is used not as a hammer but as a rubbing, pressing instrument. Get the assembly into clamps immediately after rollering and hammering.

With the panel securely in clamps make an inspection of all edges. Use spatula, craft knife, or even a damp towel to pick off glue ooze. Don't smear it around. It you cannot conveniently reach it, leave it until dry.

Weights and clamps. Bricks and weights are a temptation. It is easier to use weights than clamps. Small craftwork can be safely weighted.

6-7. Veneer hammer applies heavy pressure to guarantee over-all good bond between veneer and large glue-fresh panel. Should be worked zigzag down center and along edges

Fully veneered panels measuring about 9 x 12 or more should be clamped. For some glue-ups you can work a combination of clamps around the perimeter, eliminating heavy crossbearers and stacked bricks on the middle area. In this setup you must rest the panel on a brick or other support underneath to raise clamp handles off the bench; otherwise central bricks on top simply bow the middle.

Glue clean-up. When a glued assembly comes out of clamps it must be cleaned up. There will be an accumulation of small glue bubbles around the glue line. Use a thin spatula to get under and loosen these bubbles. Go after stubborn bubbles with the small chisel blade in your craft knife. Work them loose from all angles, slowly and gently. If squeeze-out has gotten on a veneer surface, the best removal method is scraping with the chisel blade. Sanding is a last resort, because sanding enough to remove glue smear is risky and not very effective until the glue has fully hardened. Scraping with patience is the best technique. Don't attack glue smears on veneer with what is customarily called a cabinet scraper, handled type, unless you first blunt the corners of the blade with a file.

Contact gluing techniques

Procedures for contact glue differ from the techniques described for white and yellow squeeze-bottle glues. Application with brush and wooden comb spreader are about the same, except that both assembly surfaces are coated with contact. After that, the methods of assembly differ.

A brief demonstration for contact glue will follow. A fraternal emblem is being prepared for mounting on a hardboard panel. (6-8)

Some craftsmen start by trimming the veneer

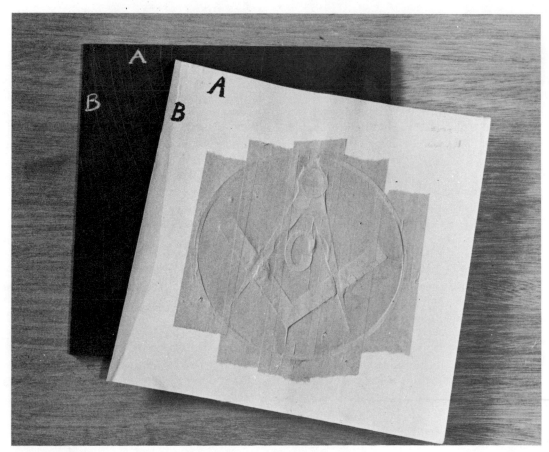

6-8. Veneer face, preassembled. Parts held with paper tape. To lay with contact glue, mark top and one side of face and hardboard panel. Trim face on these edges before assembly

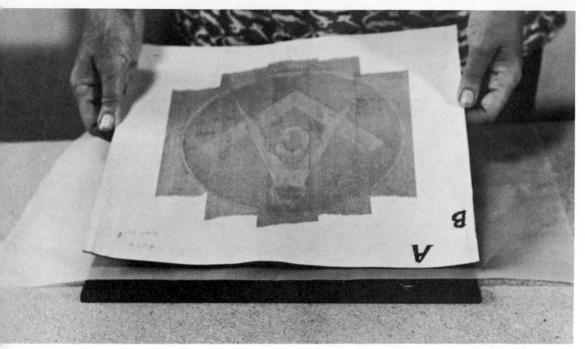

6-9. Contact glue on veneer face and panel, separated by wax paper except along top where alignment and contact are started. Marked edges A and B are easy to align evenly

face to the exact size of the mounting panel. One alternative to this system is not to trim the veneer face, and to lay it somewhat by guess and feel. One of the tricks for even easier alignment is shown.

The gum-paper side of the purchased pre-assembled veneer face is to be the final, outside face. This side is marked A for the top edge, B for one side edge. The hardboard panel is marked to match.

The veneer face which is larger than the panel is laid flat on the bench, paper side underneath. The mounting panel is laid upon the veneer and a pencil line is drawn to indicate veneer overhang. Overhang of edges A and B is next trimmed from the veneer. This simple system gives you two adjoining edges for perfect alignment and two other edges with overhang as a safety margin for trimming later.

To start the gluing, spread an even coat of contact glue on each surface. Keep them far apart. If they touch, the glue will make instant and permanent bond. Follow wait time and second coat instructions given earlier.

Test glued surfaces. When the glue allows a sheet of brown paper to slide around, without sticking, the parts are ready for assembly. Place a sheet of brown paper or wax paper over the panel, except for a slim margin of ¼ inch across the top. (6-9) Bring the veneer face to the panel. Place A and B edges in the same location. Align the corner A-B and press down. It will take hold. Move your fingers along the veneer, pressing it down on the exposed panel all along edge A. Pull the slipsheet down about ½ inch and rub the surfaces together. Keep up this procedure while making sure constantly that edge B of veneer and edge B of panel are in perfect alignment.

After full contact of veneer and panel, continue to rub down. Follow earlier instructions for using roller and hammer. Weights or clamps are advised for a few minutes to assure complete contact in all areas. Afterward, trim the remaining overhang from the other two edges. Turn the panel upside down on a smooth, clean surface and cut with a sharp craft knife. (6-10) Follow detailed instructions in chapter 13 for removing paper tape from the face.

6-10. Trimming overhang of back veneer, laid to provide balanced panel construction

7. Selecting, preparing, and cutting work veneers

Selecting. Every sheet of veneer is different, just as every tree of the same variety is unlike its family members. Your supply of veneers may include consecutive sheets; that is, sheets cut from the same flitch, next to each other. Veneer manufacturers are scrupulously careful to stack sheets in rotation as they come from the cutter and drier. If it were not for this special care, you would be unable to have two or more sheets, almost identical, for creating a wide matched panel of two or more sheets. Even your matching sheets, however, have variations which should play an important role in selection, so as not to break up a beautiful pair for a single-sheet job.

From your supply of veneer always select the sheets that fit your use. If this suggestion seems obvious, consider its full significance. Veneers are moderately costly and should be utilized to the last square foot, and in most craftwork to the last square inch. Where you can use leftovers, use them. For instance, the back of a panel for a small table top, the underside of a serving tray, or the inside surface of chest sides will never be seen. Instead of working with the largest sheets in your supply, which are the easiest to handle, try the economy of using smaller leftovers and damaged sheets. Glue joints between pieces are easily filled.

For face veneers, use your best sheets only if the intended use warrants the best. The choice of kind is largely a matter of personal taste, but there are practical factors that should not be ignored. Factors to consider are: grain characteristics where wear is important; grain and color for finishing qualities; shock resistance where a soft wood would be easily dented; stability, or tendency to warp, a quality you can judge by examining the flatness or curl of sheets in your

supply. There also is an esthetic factor: the effect of light reflection, about which you will find suggestions in chapter 15.

Viewer for small squares. When you need extra-choice figure of small area for an inset, a box lid, or craft cutout, here is a helpful aid for selecting it. Cut a rectangular hole in a piece of cardboard. Make the hole about ½ inch larger in width and length than the size of the piece you need. This allows margin for trimming. Move this viewer around on various sheets of veneer until you find exactly the quality of figure that does the most for your project. Make a pencil mark around the hole to establish cutting guidelines.

Preparing veneer for your project. Veneer sheets are not necessarily ready to glue down. From handling, transit, storage, and excessive humidity changes various sheets may need some minor repair or correction before use.

The essential thinness of veneer makes it brittle. Some kinds are much more brittle than others. Brazilian rosewood, teak, zebrano, oak, butternut, chinawood and others you will use, including the 1/40 dyed woods, require extra caution in handling. Splits generally start at the ends and run with the grain. Some, but not all, butts, burls and crotches are apt to split almost anywhere in the area of eyes and pinholes.

Mending split veneer. It is quite easy and commonplace to repair a split and go ahead as though it were perfect, except that the side you repair with tape must be the upside, or face side. Before applying finish to the face side scrape off the tape.

Gummed paper tape 1½ wide is best for mending a split. Stationery store tape will serve if you do not have veneer tape sold by craftsman suppliers. Pull the two sections of veneer together tightly at the split. Be certain they are not overlapping. Lay moistened tape down the line of split. (7-1) Press hard. Rub down for awhile. Place a heavy weight over the tape. Allow long enough for the tape to stick well. Follow further instructions given for book matching.

Curled veneer. There are factors within your control that increase the curly nature of some veneers. How you store them, where and under what conditions of heat and humidity are the correctable factors. The nature of burls and the manner of manufacture are factors contributing to curl, which of course are beyond your control. What you can do is to flatten the curled veneers before you cut out your work sheets, or after you cut, at your option.

How to flatten veneers. If time permits, start three days before you are ready to use the veneer. One day is imperative, three are better. Sprinkle each buckled sheet very lightly with water. The best way to prevent over-wetting is to dip a whiskbroom in a pan of water and flick water on the veneer. (7-2) One or two slaps on the other hand will sprinkle all the water you should apply. Lay the moistened sheets on a flat surface. Sandwich each veneer sheet between brown paper. Clean grocery bags, seams cut away, make fine veneer blankets, better than newspaper which could ink-stain light veneers. Place a flat panel on top. Add heavy weights gradually and evenly over the top panel. The more weight, the better. Leave the assembly for 24 hours. Then change the blankets for fresh, dry sheets. Repeat again the next day. Remove only when you are immediately ready to use the veneers. For this reason there is an advantage in having cut your work-size veneers before placing them in the flattening press. Now they are ready to use.

Veneer should never be moistened just before use. Unless veneer is dry when glue is applied it is apt to shrink excessively and cause splits or blisters in the finished panel. This is one of the most important rules in veneering.

Backing for unruly veneer. The moisten/press system described for taking the curl out of veneer is effective perhaps 99% of the time. It probably will work every time for you. Try it, but if the curl persists you may have to resort to

7-1. Split in striped padauk is being mended with paper tape on face side. Split will never be noticed

7-2. Curled veneer, like piece of poplar burl, flattens out when sprinkled lightly and weighted for overnight

this next method. This extra step is for the rare sheet of burl or the extra-large sheet of pony-tail crotch mahogany that is too precious to take the chance of gluing down, only to have it start splitting when dry.

Select a sheet of flat, straight-grained veneer of the same size. Plain mahogany is a good choice. Poplar and sycamore are not quite as stable. Use this piece as backing for the curled sheet. Glue it with Titebond or something else stronger than white glue. Lay it with the grain running parallel to the face veneer. When this panel comes out of clamps it is ready for immediate use as a face veneer. Glue it to a prepared panel just as you would handle any single-thick face veneer.

Alternate backing technique. All experts agree that veneers with a marked tendency to split need backing. Some experts do not completely agree with the technique of backing these extra-brittle veneers with a backing sheet running with the grain of the face veneer, although many craftsmen use the pre-backing method described above. The alternate method requires, in fact demands. a crossband sheet. 1/28 poplar is a good choice, laid cross grain on the core ahead of the brittle face veneer.

Cutting veneer with a saw. The handy little veneer saw (7-3) is the best tool for cutting veneer against a straightedge. It cuts straight, resists the pull of stubborn grain—a most essential quality—and does not chip edges along the kerf. It has no set, so that it leaves only a narrow kerf. A dovetail saw is reasonably good as a second choice.

Cutting veneer with a knife. An inexpensive craft knife belongs in the tool box of veneer craftsmen. It is often easier to reach than the saw and sometimes just as satisfactory. However, it has a strong tendency to follow grain, more pronounced on some woods such as dyed woods, oak and other woods with alternating hard and soft streaks of irregular grain. It is indispensible for cutting curved shapes. Always fit it with the sharply-pointed, tapering blade. Always cut from an edge toward the center of the piece. (7-4) Back up the cutting line with clear tape, on the underside of the veneer, if you are working with veneer that chips easily. If in doubt, back it up anyway.

Creating designs with veneers. As earlier related, veneer sheets are available in consecutive sheets. This practice gives you two or more sheets of almost identical design. When you fold open two consecutive sheets you are viewing what is called book matched—you opened the leaves of the book. If you buy 4 sheets of Brazilian rosewood, for example, you have 2 symmetrical pairs. (7-5) They will create one standard design. Typical other combinations are end to end, 4-piece match in a variety of positions, diamond designs, herringbone patterns, radiating quadrants, and many somewhat bizarre, outmoded creations. As a demonstration of the simplest form of matched design, a 2-piece match of Brazilian rosewood is shown step-by-step as it becomes a matched panel for a serving tray.

Making a 2-piece book match. Start by laying side by side the two sheets you have selected. Open them book fashion. Inspect for quality, defects and whether the combined pieces meet your requirements for size after the inside edges have been trimmed and the outside edges squared. The next step is to join them together, but first you must cut straight inside edges for a perfect joint.

Jointing inside edges. Lay one piece on the other. Align edges with enough margin to make certain of getting a straight edge the entire length of each sheet. Using a steel square as a straightedge, cut through both sheets with your veneer saw. (7-6) Now you have a reasonably good jointing edge, but not perfect.

Homemade jointing jig. The jig illustrated (7-7) was made of two pieces of hard maple 1⅜ x 3 x 28. It was bored for two carriage bolts and wing nuts. The two pieces of rosewood were clamped in the jig with the cut edges projecting slightly and evenly. A plane set very shallow, with just a perceptible bite, was run across the edges. When the veneer is flush, and cannot be felt projecting, the jointing has been accomplished.

The jig could just as well be run over a power jointer. Shaving the jig evenly on a jointer does not damage it. Smaller pieces of veneer may be jointed by simply clamping them between two boards in a bench vise.

7-3. Veneer saw cuts straighter than knife, which
follows irregular grain. Brazilian rosewood shown

7-4. Knife has little tendency to follow grain in makori
example because cutting is cross-grain

7-5. Book matching veneers starts when you buy consecutive sheets like these rosewood pairs

7-6. First step for two-piece book match panel is trimming one edge of two stacked sheets

7-7. Homemade jointing jig holds both pieces while
two edges are jointed even with plane

7-8. Perfectly jointed edges taped together on face
side. Now ready for gluing to panel

7-9. This is the final panel made by book matching a pair of consecutive sheets of Brazilian rosewood. The method which was demonstrated produced an almost invisible center joint. This panel was made into a serving tray by mitering walnut molding around the edges

Taping the joint. The two pieces of veneer are now laid on the workboard with jointed edges together. To insure a tight joint, veneer pins may be driven into both pieces about one inch away from the joint. Slant the pins toward the joint to bring the two edges together. Pinholes are easily filled later. Close the joint with gum tape as described for taping splits. (7-8) Turn over the assembly, flex the center joint open very slightly, run a stream of glue along this joint. Brush the glue across the joint. Close the book. Smeared glue along the joint harms nothing. This is the side you glue down.

From here on, treat the assembled match as a single face veneer. Glue it to a panel with the tape side up. Remove the face tape as directed in chapter 13 on Finishing.

Completed rosewood panel. The demonstration of how to make a book-matched veneer panel concludes with the finished Brazilian rosewood panel. (7-9) The illustrated sequence shows the comparative ease with which a handsome panel can be created. The center joint is hardly visible. This veneer came from a tree of small diameter. The veneer is necessarily not very wide, and the only way to provide a wide rosewood panel is to join narrow sheets together as shown here. This example shows how impor-

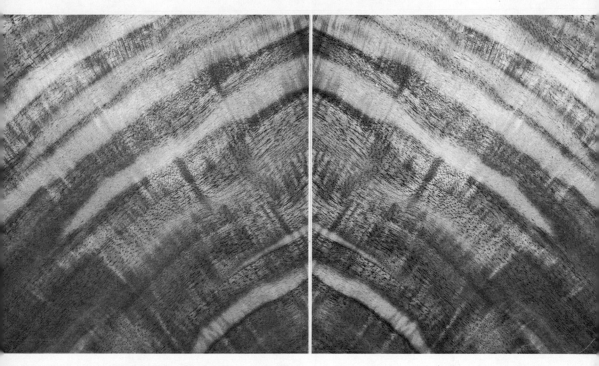

7-10. Fancy matched panels include rainbow created by cutting two pieces on bias from consecutive sheets of butt walnut. Diamond and reverse-diamond are more frequently made

tant it is to learn the fairly simple techniques of book-matching veneers.

Fancier matches. The only limitations on design matching possibilities are the craftsman's own imagination and desire to be creative. This fancy-match demonstration is not meant to encourage bizarre creations which have been in and out of fashion since man first discovered that a rich world of design could be cut out of trees.

Large exotic matches are tiresome, but fancy matches on small table tops, serving trays, and a single door on a cabinet can lift the commonplace object to a level of tasteful decor. An example (7-10) is the pair of walnut crotch veneers illustrated. Two consecutive veneer sheets were cut on the bias to create an arc from each sheet. They were then placed together so each arc met its neighbor and created a half circle. This demonstration suggests many other ways to create matched panels by cutting veneer sheets at angles, rather than following the method of straight-cut book matching.

Special handling. When you are preparing a sheet of bird's-eye maple for gluing, examine both sides. Identify the underside and glue that side against the panel. Here is what happens to bird's-eye to make it a veneer that demands special handling. (7-11)

Bird's-eye maple is not considered a burl; yet it has an abundance of eyes like a burl. Sheets of bird's-eye vary considerably in the size and frequency of the eyes, but a common characteristic is prevalent in all sheets. The eyes appear to have a different structure on the two sides of a sheet. This difference is perceptible on close examination if you know what to look for. The difference was produced by cutting at the veneer plant.

Bird's-eye maple is customarily rotary cut. A log is mounted horizontally in a lathe. As the log rotates against a stationary knife, a continuous sheet of veneer is sheared from the log. The sheet is necessarily flexed as it comes off the log and is pulled away by a system of rollers.

Flexing stretches and expands the underside

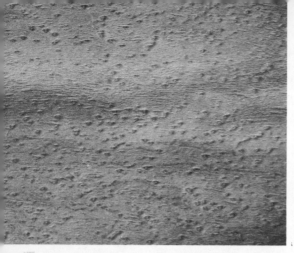

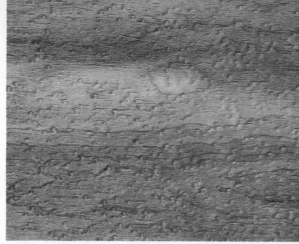

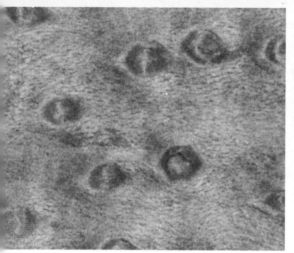

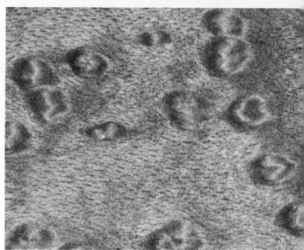

7-11. Bird's-eye maple has different texture on its two sides. Eyes on the underside, the side to glue down, come to peaks. You can see and feel difference. Bottom photo shows enlarged view

This is the topside of bird's-eye maple. Smoother to the touch. Eyes are cratered, firmly embedded. Use this as the face side of a panel. Bottom photo shows enlarged view of upper photo

of the sheet while it compresses the topside. Flexing causes lathe checks on the underside, and it pops the eyes out just a perceptible amount on this underside.

On the underside of bird's-eye you can see and feel peaks at the points of the eye. On the topside you can see, but not really feel, craters at the points of the eyes. This is more than an interesting observation. It is important to the veneer craftsman. The underside, with peaks, should be glued down; otherwise you may find some of the eyes popping out after the veneer has been glued to a panel. Take the extra moment to identify the underside of the sheet the next time you handle bird's-eye maple.

Storing veneers properly can minimize their faults. Much of the splitting and warping that

takes place after you bring veneers into your shop can be avoided by improved handling and storage.

Provide a safe, out-of-the-way storage space for veneers. Frequent handling to move them out of the way momentarily is a costly practice. Store veneers flat on wide shelves or tables. A platform under a worktable is one of the many good storage places. Keep veneers flat. Leave them in the cardboard shipping cartons they came in. Place a plywood panel or other weighting device on top. Be sure the ends and edges of veneer sheets are as even as possible. In this way they somewhat protect each other. A cool basement, even though mildly damp, is a better storage area than a hot furnace room or attic. Do not store veneers on end.

8. Clamps, presses, and weights

Only one type of glue you will use requires no clamps, presses or weights. It is contact glue. For all other gluing of veneer work you need clamps. Four styles of clamps are illustrated. (8-1) Your need for these is, of course, entirely dependent upon your work. You do not necessarily need all four.

Spring clamps. This quick, one-handed clamp is ideal for whatever small jobs it can get its jaws on, providing that no great amount of pressure is required. For instance, a veneer patch near a panel's edge can be glued and spring-clamped with a protective pad to avoid jaw marks on the veneer. The size clamp shown, with a 2-inch open jaw, is the most practical. Two are recommended.

C-clamps. This style of clamp is indispensible. The size illustrated is known as 3-inch, indicating jaw opening. The next size is 4-inch. The extra opening is seldom needed but the extra depth of throat is more than welcome. The only problem is that the larger one costs about twice as much. Whatever you buy, get them in even numbers so that pressure can be dependably equalized across a panel. On small jobs, say 7 inches wide, the 3-inch size can be used without crossbearers, and with reasonable safety on most woods if you have firm cauls. You can spread the pressure a little by placing 2x2 squares of ¼-inch ply or hardboard as pads under each jaw. This is good practice at all times to avoid jaw dents in the caul.

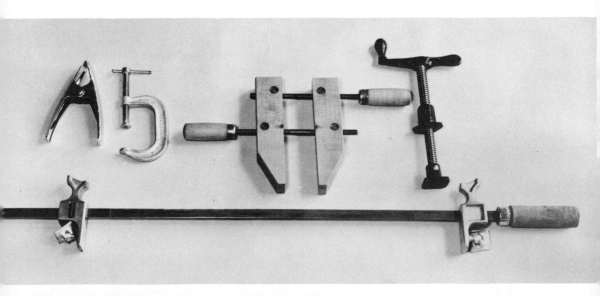

8-1. Styles of clamps most useful in veneering. Spring type is temporary work holder. C-clamps best when using crossbearers. Handscrews have deepest throat. Veneer press screw. Bar clamp

8-2. Angle irons provide best method for applying central pressure. Never bow or flex, replace heavy wooden crossbearers, eliminate need for big clamps, and usually can be picked up at junkyard

Wood crossbearers. Conventional woodworking practice calls for wood crossbearers. Their purpose is to apply pressure at the center of the work. The trouble you will have with wood crossbearers is compound; that is, if they are less than 2x4's they will bow at the center when clamped at the ends, and if they are 2x4's you must buy much larger clamps. Cabinetmakers sometimes put a plane to crossbearers and taper them slightly toward each end so that the center is raised to compensate for the bowed ends. Still, you need larger clamps. Furthermore, if you taper the crossbearers too much you lighten up on pressure near the ends. Make only a slight taper with your plane, and check each crossbearer against the others to assure uniform tapering on all members. Chapter 15 reveals an even simpler trade trick!

Simplified crossbearers. An easy solution to the problem of crossbearers seems reasonably well concluded by the novel introduction of angle-iron crossbearers to supplant wood. (8-2) Angle iron does not bow. It is far stronger than flat steel. And it has so little thickness that 3-inch C-clamps are entirely adequate. Angle-iron crossbearers demonstrated are ¼ x 1½ x 24. If the local junkyard cannot locate them, go to a welding shop.

Handscrews. This double-spindled wood clamp is the tool of a thousand uses. With angle-iron crossbearers and C-clamps you can get along without handscrews, but they are a great convenience and they have more reach and more pressure than C-clamps. Buy them in even numbers. The size known as No. 0 opens to 4½ inches and has a throat depth of 4 inches. This is

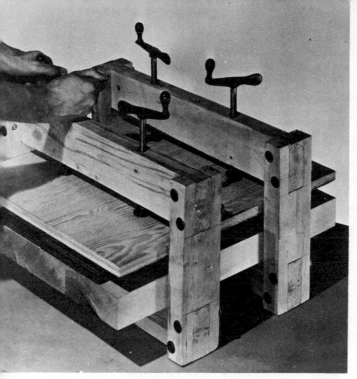

8-3. Veneer presses are clamping frames. You build as many as you think you will need. The least number is two as illustrated. Press screws come in two sizes. The construction drawing below shows details for making a frame and bed. 8-4. Large frame illustrated was built to take four press screws

a handy size, but No. 1 has a 5-inch throat and costs less than a dollar more. Extra depth is frequently welcomed. The more you accustom yourself to handling handscrews, the more uses you find. If they are new tools in your hands, discover the tricks in handling them revealed in chapter 15.

Veneer press. This equipment is over-rated as an essential for home shop veneering. It is a cumbersome piece of equipment to store, not cheap to build, and used infrequently in the average hobby shop. One veneer press frame is not very useful, although it can become the center clamping device for a panel when the two ends

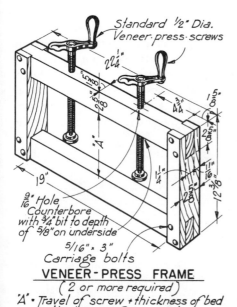

Standard ½" Dia. Veneer-press-screws

22¼"

3¾"

1⅝"

2⅝"

1¼"

1″/16″

12⅜"

19″

⅞/16″ Hole Counterbore with ¾"bit to depth of ⅝"on underside

5/16″ × 3″ Carriage bolts

VENEER-PRESS FRAME
(2 or more required)
"A" - Travel of screw + thickness of bed + thickness of one caul

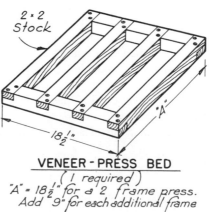

2 × 2 Stock

18½"

"A"

VENEER-PRESS BED
(1 required)
"A" = 18½" for a 2 frame press.
Add "9" for each additional frame

NOTE: Two cauls are also required. These may be ¾" plywood or glued up from ¾" boards and each faced on one side only with hardwood, fiber board, sheet metal or ¼"plywood. Make same length and width as the bed. One may be fastened to bed if desired

(8-5)

8-6. Weights provide a quick and easy way to apply pressure to glued work. Plastic bags and paper bags prevent scratching of veneer. Concrete block is useful if perfectly flat, not warped

are being clamped by conventional methods. Ordinarily the smallest number of frames for clamping panels is two. (8-3) The largest manageable collection for the home shop is about four frames. (8-4)

A veneer press is admittedly a reliable clamping device. For those who wish to build the frames, construction details are given here for frames that take panels up to 18 inches square. (8-5) Press screws may be purchased from your woodworking materials supplier. You also will have to make a veneer press bed as a bottom platform and two ¾ ply panels for a double-top caul.

Buy the press screws before starting the frame, to make certain of matching your construction to the screws. The frame shown here is based on ½-inch press screws. If you buy the heavier 11/16 screws increase frame members from 2⅝ to 3⅝ to resist the heavier pressure.

Weights. Panels up to about 2 square feet, approximately 15 inches square, can be glued successfully without clamps. Heavy weights are reliable substitutes. This does not mean that weights are better than clamps, just cheaper and quicker to put into action. An assortment of bricks and heavy iron weights puts all the weight you need on top of a flat caul board. (8-6) Plastic bags or paper bags, leftovers from produce and groceries, prevent scratches on cauls, table, floors and work sheets of veneer when you lay bag-protected bricks temporarily on these various surfaces, as you surely will do from time to time.

9. Simplified techniques for craftwork veneering

Where to start? Beautiful serving trays, inlaid boxes, chessboards, major furniture restorations, and other eye-catching projects offer big rewards to the veneer craftsman. These projects are not hard to accomplish when you follow the modern, simplified methods demonstrated throughout this book.

Many woodworking readers will start with the most appealing work illustrated, complete it easily, and go right on to greater achievements with veneer. However, if you happen to be a beginner and have never worked with veneer, a more appropriate start could be made on something as easy as a set of coasters. (9-1)

Coasters were chosen as a pilot project because they lend themselves to a quick demonstration of the first two basic techniques in veneering: how to cut veneer; and how to glue veneer. When completed, the coasters make useful home accessories or welcomed gifts, not just an exercise. The coaster project will enable you to put into practice the techniques learned in foregoing chapters.

Core stock. The first step is to provide squares of core stock not larger than 4 inches. This size permits economical layout of two veneer faces, grain on the diagonal, on a 6 x 12 sheet of veneer. (9-2)

9-1. Striped veneer, in this example, zebrano, was chosen for the simplest possible pilot project. The demonstration, resulting in a useful gift set of coasters, shows basic veneering techniques

9-2. Old coaster set of thin plywood provided core stock. Other thin woods are just as suitable

Because a coaster that buckles would be intolerable, you should select core stock that will remain stable. One of the best is ⅛ basswood. Second choice, ⅛ poplar. Third choice, 3/16 hardboard, which is stable but somewhat heavy for coasters. Cut the cores to size and round the corners. If you are using a core of wood, cut the core with grain on the diagonal. This enables you to turn the core 90 degrees and have the grain running at right angles to face and back veneer. For the demonstration a pair of 30-year-old airplane plywood coasters was used as core stock.

Veneer for your first projects. One of the handiest starter kits for practicing and perfecting your work habits is the Introductory Veneer Kit illustrated. (9-3) It contains 4 kinds of veneer, 2 square feet of each kind. One coaster veneered both sides takes less than ½ foot. An attractive

coaster set could be veneered on one side with striped veneer and backed with leaf or mottle figured veneer.

Cutting veneer. The first of the basic techniques is cutting. For larger veneer work, the veneer saw is the recommended tool. For cutting a small square, the craft knife is easier to handle. (9-4) Cut from the edge toward the center to avoid splitting the edge. The pencil layout is oversize to allow a small margin for trimming later.

Gluing. Two ways to glue the veneer to the core will be shown. You will need both methods when you undertake a variety of veneer work. Shown first is liquid glue which requires weighting or clamping. Titebond, which we call yellow glue, is used here. White glue could have been used; the method would have been the same.

Spread yellow glue on the core, not on the veneer. (9-5) Allow 3 minutes for it to develop tack, then lay the glue-fresh side of the core on the square of veneer. (9-6) Turn the assembly over, face up, and roller the veneer hard to assure firm, even contact all over.

Lay the assembly between two small caul boards. Place about 3 bricks or equivalent on top. Leave overnight. The next day trim off the overhanging veneer with your craft knife. To do this safely lay the assembly with veneer face down on a cutting board. Cut around the core

9-3. Quickest way to get started veneering a set of coasters is with kit containing variety of veneer in squares that cut economically into standard four-inch coasters. Cut straight or diagonal grain

9-4. Cuts made across diagonal grain with craft knife with very little danger of splitting. However, if cut were being made along straight grain of zebrano the veneer saw would make a better cut

lightly at first, then make somewhat heavier cuts. Don't try to cut through with one stroke. You will chip the veneer.

The veneer square for the first coaster was cut oversize at all edges. For easy assembly and visible alignment, so you can watch the align-ment, you should cut the second veneer square differently. Leave margin on right and bottom edges; no margin on left and top edges.

On the second coaster, contact glue is used to illustrate how this method differs from the gluing method used for the first coaster.

9-5. This is first of two gluing methods shown for coasters. Here, yellow glue is spread on core

9-6. With yellow glue becoming tacky on under-side of core, lay core on oversize veneer face

Spread contact glue on both surfaces to be joined; that is, on the core and on the veneer. (9-7) Keep these two members far apart. If they touch, they will stick. Allow 30 minutes or more for the glue to lose all of its tack. Test the tack by trying to slide a sheet of brown paper across the glued surface. If it does not slide freely allow more drying time. When the glued surface passes the paper test, apply a second coat of contact glue on each surface. Again allow time to dry completely.

Lay a slipsheet, brown paper or wax paper, over the core, leaving a visible margin of ¼ inch across the top and ⅛-inch margin down the left side.

Place the veneer over the core. Align the two top edges and the two left edges, both of which were left exposed by the slipsheet. (9-8) Press veneer against core. Bond is immediate and permanent. Now pull the slipsheet down about ½ inch and press again. Proceed like this until the slipsheet is removed and contact is complete.

Roller the veneer hard against the core to assure overall firm, even contact. (9-9) Place the assembly under weights for 30 minutes. Trim off the two overhanging edges and gently sand all edges. While holding the coaster upright, veneer face toward you, work your sanding block across the edge and away from you to avoid chipping. Don't draw the sanding block across the veneer edge toward you.

For balanced construction, preventing warp, you should next lay a square of veneer on the back of the core. Lay the grain at right angles to the grain of the core, parallel to the face grain.

Brush or spray several coats of a urethane varnish like Wood-glo on the completed coasters. Be sure to finish the edges well to prevent moisture penetration.

How to make a chessboard

One of the important techniques practiced while making a coaster in the pilot project demonstration can be put to use on a chessboard. You watched the trick of visible alignment when laying veneer on a core with contact glue. Follow the same method now.

The chessboard veneer face is pre-assembled. You buy it ready to glue down. On the back is a crisscross of gum tape holding the chessboard squares and border together.

9-7. Second gluing method is started. Spread contact glue on veneer face and on core. Wait to dry
9-8. Surfaces spread with contact glue, now dry, separated by slip-sheet except at aligning edges
9-9. Rollering, a vital technique. Roller veneer hard against core to assure over-all firm contact

Start by procuring a ½-inch flakeboard panel 18 inches square for the core. The chessboard face comes oversize with an allowance for trimming to 18 inches square. Apply walnut wood trim around the edges of the panel. This is easy to do after you examine the illustrations in the chapter on edging.

Next, trim the overhang from top and lefthand edges of the chessboard face. These are the two edges you will align with the panel when laying the face on the panel, brown paper slipsheet between. (9-10) This is exactly the same way you saw the coaster laid up. The chessboard face, however, has a paper backing. Lay the veneer with the paper side up. Roller the veneer hard to assure firm, even contact all over. (9-11) After the assembly has set for two or three days, remove paper backing as described in chapter 13.

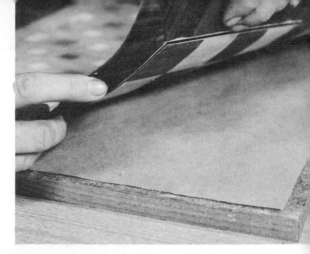

9-10. Laying chessboard veneer face on panel. Slipsheet leaves top, side exposed for alignment

How to veneer small boxes

Unfinished basswood boxes offer an easy way to start another worthwhile veneering project. Readymade boxes are sold in many shapes and sizes. The rectangular box chosen for veneering measures 11 inches long. The lid is hinged. (9-12) Veneering this box involves the two basic techniques demonstrated when making the coaster set; namely, cutting and gluing small pieces of veneer. There now are more pieces to handle, but the methods are the same.

The completed model (9-13) features an eagle inlay, but this decorative treatment is not essential. You can produce a handsome box covered with walnut veneer without undertaking the inlay. You simply cover the lid with a single square of walnut veneer. For those craftsmen who care to try the inlay, a very simple method will be shown after the steps in box veneering have been completed.

The first step is removal of hinges. It is impractical to lay veneer around the hinges. Use a screwdriver to get under the hinge to pry it loose. (9-14) Slip a protective scrap of veneer under the tip to prevent the tool from denting the box.

Most of these unfinished hinged boxes are assembled with drive hinges. Throw the hinges away after you have removed them. Drive hinges are originally put in by machine. You will have a difficult time trying to drive them in by hand methods. The points will buckle under and

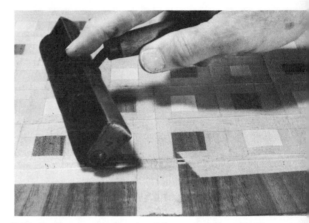

9-11. Roller veneer face hard for over-all contact. Allow glue several days to set, then remove tape

9-12. Unpainted boxes sold in craft stores offer a quick way to start a popular veneering project

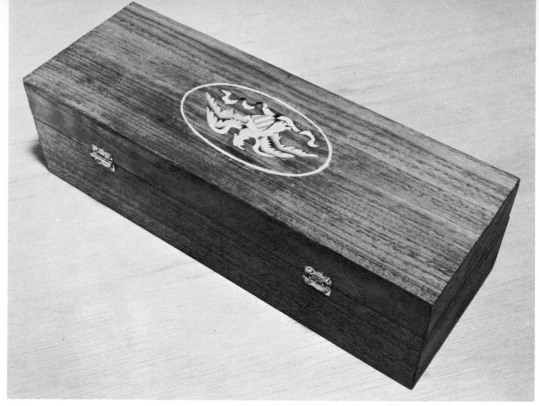

9-13. Box veneered with walnut was inlaid to show how much a simplified technique can add

You now probably will not end up with a tight, aligned fit between box and lid. Buy a replacement set of small screw hinges. They are easy to install.

You now have two box parts to veneer: the shallower lid and the deeper base. To avoid possible confusion of parts, consider them as separate projects. Starting with the lid, cut two long strips of walnut veneer for front and back. Cut two short strips for the ends. Make every strip about 3/16 oversize at every edge. That

means to cut each strip ⅜ larger than the lid surface to be covered.

Mark each walnut strip on the glue side. For instance, one lid end and the veneer strip for that end are marked AI. For the other end, AII. To determine which side is to be the glue side, examine each veneer strip for inherent blemishes, knife marks made in manufacture and for best figure. Mark the poorest side, and that will be the glue side.

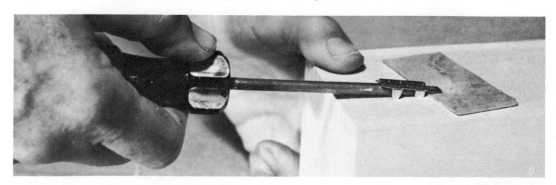

9-14. Remove drive hinges and discard. Replace later with screw hinges. Protect box from tool tip with scrap veneer. Lid and box will be covered with walnut veneer, then inlaid and re-hinged

9-15. Cut walnut strips oversize for trimming later. Lid shown at left. Box, right. Order of gluing to conceal most edge grain is back, 2 ends, front. Clamp with cauls inside and out

Follow the same procedure of selecting, marking, and cutting strips for the base. You now have 4 strips of walnut for each box section. (9-15) There is one more piece to cut, the walnut square for the top of the lid. A square for the underside of the base is strictly optional. It is not needed. A piece of felt glued to the bottom might be more practical.

Which strip goes on first? The general rule is to apply last what you see first. To follow this rule for veneering the box you would proceed in this order: 1, back; 2, ends; 3, front; 4, top of lid. If you decide to veneer the bottom, you would lay it before any other piece. What this order accomplishes is to conceal as much end grain and edge grain of the veneer as possible.

Gluing veneer to the box. White glue was used for the model project, but yellow glue or contact glue would be just as satisfactory. Your choice should be based on how you can work out the clamping arrangements. Weights would be impractical. If clamping appears difficult or too slow, waiting for one panel to dry before another can be glued, use the faster method afforded by contact glue.

Simplified inlay

To decorate the box lid by following the simplest inlay method, start with a readymade veneer face. The American spread eagle was chosen for the model. When you were laying walnut veneer on the box, your last piece was the square

9-16. Sandwich walnut square for box lid between two balsa squares to make saw pad. Trace eagle oval

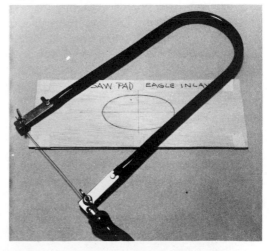

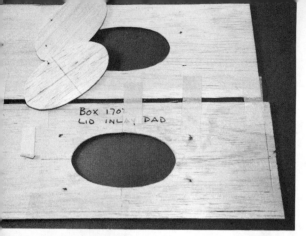

9-17. Bore blade hole within oval. Cut oval with a fret saw. This method cuts oval opening in walnut

9-18. Glue walnut square on box lid. This simple technique avoids difficult routering for inlay

you cut for the box lid. The inlay trick here is to cut out an oval at the center of that piece of veneer before you lay it with glue.

There are two ways to cut the oval opening. To cut it with a craft knife draw two extended center lines on the veneer. Locate center lines on the eagle. Lay the eagle on the veneer and trace it to create your cutting guideline. Cut with a craft knife.

To cut the oval opening in the manner many professionals use for much more complicated

9-19. Top, glue eagle inlay, paper side up, in lid recess. Allow 24 hours or more for glue to harden. Moisten gum paper lightly, wait a moment to soften. Center, scrape gum paper and residue with chisel. Bottom, fill joint around eagle inlay with mix of powdered wood filler and white glue. Sand when dry

inlays, use the fretsaw pad method. Layer the square of walnut veneer between two pieces of balsa. Lay out the oval on center lines drawn on the top member of the saw pad. (9-16) Drill a hole for the saw blade inside the oval and cut with a fret saw. Open the pad (9-17) and lay the walnut veneer with glue on the box lid. (9-18) Glue the eagle veneer face, paper side up, in the recessed walnut lid. Moisten and scrape off all gum tape. (9-19) To perfect the joint around the inlay, press in filler, fine sawdust mixed with white glue.

By following the inlaying method shown for the eagle box lid, you have saved yourself a considerable amount of exacting work. The alternative method requires a portable electric router. You would lay the walnut square, without oval opening, on the box lid. You would then cut an oval recess with the router, and this is far from easy. To make an accurate routered recess you should make up a template to guide the router. It becomes obvious that the inlaying method illustrated was about as simple, and time-saving, a method as a person could expect to find.

The next time you undertake a woodworking project involving inlay you might try to adapt the simplified inlaying method to your project. You might even consider laying a fresh sheet of veneer over the entire top of a small table or serving tray just to save yourself the harder task of routering a recess.

Veneering a box, with variation

Another unfinished craft box, bought ready-made as a holder for a standard box of facial tissue, serves as a model for a different decorative treatment. (9-20) The completed box with an inlaid border is illustrated in chapter 2 in a group of projects showing ways to capitalize on your veneering skills.

The veneer chosen for this demonstration is one of the most beautiful woods, African cherry, known in the trade as makori. It is deep, dark reddish brown with a special quality for reflecting a moving sheen of light.

The working method you followed for veneering the walnut box can be put to work again for this larger box. Lay out and cut veneer squares slightly oversize for two ends and two sides. (9-21)

9-20. Unpainted box, slotted top and slip bottom, holds facial tissue box. To be veneered and inlaid

9-21. Silky red-brown makori veneer cut oversize for ends and sides will make attractive holder

9-22. Apply mahogany stain around rim of opening to allow veneer edge to be set back unnoticed

9-23. Lay veneer on ends first. Cut overhang and gently smooth cut edges with fine sandpaper

9-25. To inlay banding as fillet strip, cut veneer strips flush on inside edge, overhang on outside

Before actually veneering the box, brush mahogany stain around the edge of the oval opening. (9-22) This is the simplest way of minimizing the raw edge of the opening. It also conceals a slight setback of the veneer. If veneer comes too close to the working edge, tissue may sometime catch a sliver and damage the veneer.

Select whichever gluing method you consider is most convenient, remembering that white glue and yellow glue require clamping, whereas contact glue eliminates clamping and permits the work to progress faster. Glue one panel at a time. Let it harden sufficiently to work with safely. Trim the overhang from that panel and sand the edge (9-23) before you apply the next panel. Follow this procedure until sides and ends have been glued and trimmed.

Preparing the top. Veneering the top of this box has no foregoing precedent in this book. The method to be demonstrated now was developed long ago to simplify the use of inlay banding when it is located within the veneered area, not at

9-24. Inlay banding comes in variety of designs and widths. Style for box, fourth from right

the edge as an outside border. Marquetarians employ this method when they insert a fillet strip around a picture.

When you buy the box, also buy a strip of narrow banding. For the model, 3/16 was chosen. A wide selection of banding of many styles and widths is available (9-24) but nothing wider than ¼ would be appropriate for the small area of this box.

Measure the box you have purchased. Decide how wide an outside border you can use. The trimmed border on the model is ⅞ wide. Make a pencil layout on the top. Cut the border strips slightly oversize in width and length. Because the inside edge of each strip is a final edge, joining the inlay banding, the veneer saw was used to cut the strips. (9-25) It is somewhat easier to control on twisting grain than a knife would be.

Turn back to the layout on the box. Place the strips in outside position, add a length of banding next. Lay out and measure the remaining center area to determine the dimension for the center square. Cut it to exact size. It has no overhang.

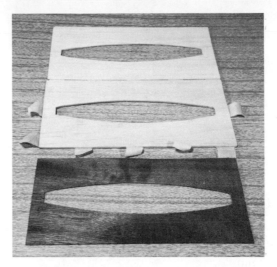

9-26. For smoothest edge, use saw pad method to cut center slot in veneer. Use knife if preferred

9-27. Trial fit all parts for veneering box top. Sand if needed to perfect joints. Make pencil guidelines for center panel. Glue it down first. Fit banding next, ends overlapping for mitering

Cutting the oval. You can cut the center opening with your craft knife if you think you can make a clean, even edge. To locate the opening accurately, one way is to tape the veneer square in position on the top, turn the box upside down, reach inside and trace the opening onto the veneer.

If you prefer the saw pad method introduced for the eagle inlay in the walnut box, make a balsa saw pad the same size as the veneer. Tape the top member of the saw pad in position on the box. Turn the box upside down and trace the opening onto the saw pad to provide a cutting line for the saw. Layer the veneer between top and bottom pads and cut the opening. (9-26) With either cutting method, knife or saw, cut outside the line so that you make the opening the slightest bit larger than your pattern line.

Banding. Cut the banding ½ inch longer than the size of the center veneer panel. The extra length allows for mitering later. You now have all parts for the top. (9-27)

Start veneering the top by gluing down the center panel on layout lines drawn earlier. Next, glue down one long banding strip tightly against the center panel. Omit glue from the ends until later. Use tape to hold banding in position. Lay a short strip of banding next and allow it to overlap the long strip at the corner. With your craft knife make a miter cut through both pieces of banding. (9-28) Slide glue under the mitered ends to complete the banding. (9-29)

Outside border. Lay a border strip tightly against the banding and let it overhang at ends and edge. Wax paper is a helpful aid in bordering. (9-30) Slip a little piece of paper under the end of the border. Spread glue only up to the paper. Put another piece between the two border strips where they overlap. After you cut the miter through the two border strips, you can remove the veneer waste because you did not glue it down. Now slip glue under the miters.

9-28. Top, lay wax paper under overlap to keep it from gluing down. Protect center when cutting miter.

9-29. Center, remove wax paper and glue down ends of banding. Box is ready for outside border strips.

9-30. Bottom, again lay wax paper under miter area. Glue end strips, then side strips

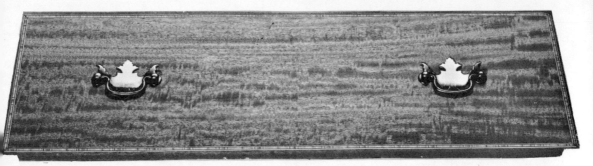

9-31. Another simplified inlay technique, how to lay any width of outside border without difficult routing and chiseling. Mahogany mottle veneer laid on drawer front. Border is banding

Veneering and inlaying a drawer front

This demonstration is intended to present a simplified way to veneer a solid panel and lay narrow banding around the edge. (9-31) This is a drawer front, but the technique could apply as well to a table top. The method must be entirely different from the tissue box veneering technique because now the outside edging is not a piece of veneer you can overhang and then trim to panel size. You cannot trim banding.

Instead of following the method shown here, it may sound simpler to lay a short sheet of veneer in the center and then lay the banding strips around it. The difficulty with that system lies in the almost impossible task of getting the large center piece of veneer exactly squarely laid on the board and getting an exactly uniform rabbet around the edge for the banding.

The project starts with a piece of ¾ x 7½ x 24 whitewood intended as a drawer front. Ends were rabbeted and all edges were covered with wood trim. Notice that the wood trim was aligned with the inside rabbet edge of the ends. The overhang of trim sticks out where you can trim it off. (9-32) You could not conveniently trim overhang along the inside rabbet edge.

Mahogany mottle veneer was chosen for the drawer front. The first step is cutting it to size. Select the side you want for face side. Lay the veneer, face side down, on a smooth, clean workboard or benchtop. Place the wood panel on top of the veneer and trace around it. Trim one long edge and one end to the line you drew on the veneer. These trimmed, flush edges will be your aligning edges. This is the method you followed in earlier projects when laying veneer with con-

tact glue. You should use contact glue here, too, when the parts are ready.

Masking tape is the important item in this trick method. You may have used masking tape to keep paint from part of a surface you were painting. Now use tape to keep glue from around the perimeter of veneer and board. (9-33)

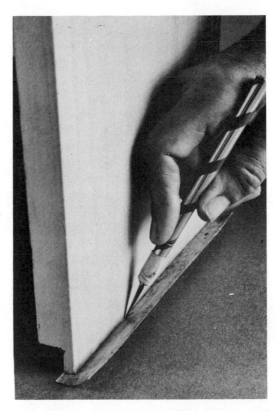

9-32. Drawer front example starts with wood trim. Lay flush with rabbet, overhang face edge

9-33. Lay masking tape around underside of veneer and face side of drawer panel. This easy trick keeps contact glue from border area

There is one thing to do before you lay the masking tape. You must lay out guidelines for the tape. On the face side of the board, measure in from the edge the width of the banding you have selected. Make a pencil line around the four edges. While remembering that you have already flush-trimmed two veneer edges, and left the other two oversize, lay out on the veneer the necessary guidelines for tape. The size of un-taped rectangular areas in the center of panel and veneer must match exactly.

Gluing. Now you are ready to spread contact glue on both surfaces to be joined. Follow earlier instructions of waiting, testing, and applying a second coat. When the glue is thoroughly dry, peel off the tape from panel and from veneer. (9-34) Lay veneer on panel in the prescribed manner. Trim the two overhanging edges of veneer.

Removing veneer border. To make the rabbet for the banding lay out on the veneer the

9-34. When contact glue dries, peel tape off veneer and drawer. Lay veneer with slipsheet

9-35. Veneer has been firmly laid on panel everywhere except around perimeter protected by tape. Now trim and remove unglued edge of veneer to produce rabbet

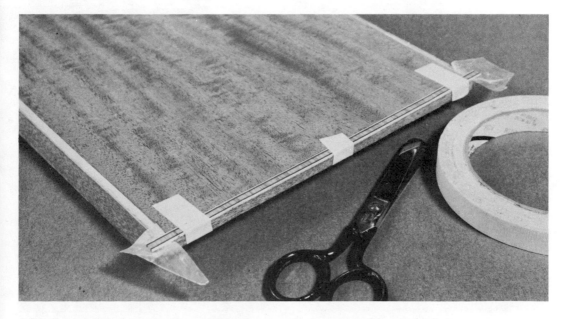

9-36. Cut banding long, to miter. Wax paper at ends. Lay with white glue which permits pressing and fitting banding against veneer. Tape substitutes for clamps

width of your banding. Make the rabbet the very slightest bit narrower than your banding, narrower by just about the width of a knife cut. This assures you of having the banding at least flush with the outside edge, or perhaps a fraction over, which can be sanded flush.

Use a reliable straightedge when trimming off the veneer to produce the rabbet. (9-35) The veneer will come off easily because there is no glue beneath it. Masking tape kept the rabbet free of glue. Check the veneer around the rabbet for good bond. Roller down the edges.

Cut the banding oversize to allow plenty of overhang for mitering. Glue the banding into the rabbet with white glue because it allows the most freedom for pushing and pressing the banding to assure a perfect joint. Banding is delicate and not die-straight, but it is flexible enough to allow this alignment procedure.

Clamp the banding with masking tape and allow glue to dry thoroughly. Slip wax paper under the ends to make mitering easier. (9-36)

9-37. Support overhanging ends of fragile banding while cutting miters with knife. Glue ends

9-38. When cutting walnut veneer to cover tin can, wind string around can and snip to length

9-39. Spread contact glue on can and veneer, then use slipsheet to separate surfaces as you contact

Veneered tin can project demonstrates that veneer is easily glued to metal

Mitering. The overhanging ends of banding are very fragile. Work out a means of support from underneath (9-37) as a precaution when cutting the miters at the corners.

Veneering a tin can

In tune with modern times, recycling a tin can is the next project. This demonstration shows that veneer can be utilized as an attractive cover material for metal as well as wood. It is a simple and useful project. Use it as a plant pot or knife holder.

Obtain a tin can without ridges. Measure the circumference with a piece of string. Cut the string and use it to mark the length of veneer square needed. Measure the can between projecting top and bottom rims. Mark and cut the veneer so its grain runs from rim to rim. (9-38) The safest veneer to use is extra-thin 1/64. Some heavier veneers could be bent around cans of larger diameter without splitting, but some veneers will split.

Spread contact glue on can and veneer. Use the slipsheet method (9-39) when you lay veneer around the can.

Box with geometrical design

Another example of how a plain, unfinished craft box can be transformed into an appealing gift box is shown by courtesy of a member of the Marquetry Society of America, Phillip Fine, Spring Valley, New York.

Every surface of this box was veneered, inside and outside. Front, back, and side panels show vertical matched grain running from top to bottom even though the lid was handled separately.

For the top panel New Guinea veneer was cut into 1-inch strips. Strips were then crosscut to make 1-inch squares. Squares were quarter-turned and assembled into an oversize veneer face on gum paper tape. The top face, applied last, was trimmed of overhang. Exposed gum tape was moistened for removal.

Craft boxes bought readymade, unpainted, are a challenge to the ingenuity of the veneer craftsman. They can be decorated with insets or overlaid cutouts. Here is one of the most popular treatments, a geometric design composed of squares of New Guinea veneer

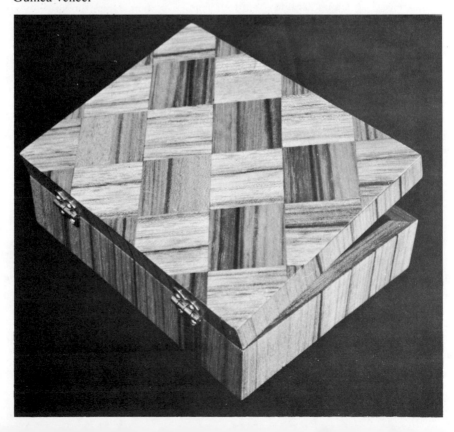

10. Making veneered panels

Everyone knows that wood warps because of changes in atmospheric humidity. When you consider just how drastic the changes are in your indoor living environment you realize the new importance of careful planning in veneering.

Indoor relative humidity in the average American climate ranges from 25 percent in cold weather to well over 60 on an ordinary cloudy summer day. This atmospheric range may alter the moisture content of wood from 6 to 11 percent. It means that a piece of 1-inch softwood 5 inches wide in a panel core could shrink 1/16 in width. If you did everything wrong when building a panel 15 inches wide you could have width shrinkage of 3/16, an intolerable condition. The example illustrates the necessity for counteracting shrinkage in panels you are going to veneer. There are ways to do it, and they will be covered here.

Balanced construction. Veneer alone is too thin for strength and too brittle to remain stable. It serves mainly as a decorative face on a stable panel. Mainly but not wholly decorative, the veneer face also helps to stabilize the other elements of the panel by contributing to balanced construction. That is the point to remember. Balanced construction. One element offsetting, or defeating, the warp tendency of its neighbor is the keynote of balanced construction.

Core of the panel. The center element of the panel is called the core. For the 70 years of plywood's development, two basic types of core construction have dominated: crisscross veneer construction consisting of layer on layer of veneer; and the solid lumber core covered on both sides with crossband veneer and then with face and back veneer. You can follow either of these construction methods in your home shop.

A third method of panel construction, the modern method, utilizes for the center element solid flakeboard, or particle board as it is often called. This is the simplest for you to use. Sometimes, however, you may need or prefer one of the other methods.

Besides the three principle systems mentioned, there are two simple alternatives which are useful to know about, even with their limitations. First, study the standard methods. Each has distinct advantages or it would not still be used.

Crisscross 3-ply method. To avoid confusion it is better to think of this as the crisscross system. Here, the term plywood will be used to mean readymade panels bought from suppliers. Crisscross starts with 3 layers of veneer; that is the minimum. (10-1) Small panels used principally in cabinet door frames, size depending upon the stable characteristics of woods you choose, can be built of 3 pieces of 1/28 veneer. Lay the center sheet with grain north/south; the face and back, east/west. Obviously this layout places each sheet at right angles to its neighbor.

Right here you meet one of the basic laws of balanced construction. The two outside sheets of this and all other laminated construction must be

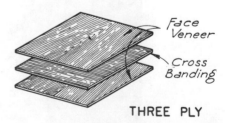

THREE PLY

10-1. Three-ply crisscross panel construction can be used when it is set into a frame for stability

as nearly alike as possible, ideally but not necessarily the same wood. They should come from the same storage area where presumably they have attained the same degree of moisture content. They must be of the same thickness. For the center core, called crossband, use 1/28 poplar or other straight-grained veneer. Poplar is the most economical.

When you glue the 3 sheets of 1/28 together, you have the thinnest panel you can safely use. There have been lampshades made of 3 layers of 1/40 but they are held in shape usually by solid framing.

To make larger panels you must make thicker panels. To do this start with a heavier core. Solid basswood and maple plywood are available in ⅛ thickness and as large as 2x4 feet. For still larger panels, use ¼ plywood smooth on both sides. Panels discussed so far are 3-ply panels.

Crisscross 5-ply method. This system makes heavier and more stable panels. (10-2) It is more work than 3-ply construction, more expensive and not always necessary. There are, however two situations which call for the extra crossbands in 5-ply construction.

First, if you are laying an unruly face veneer with a natural tendency to warp, you should play it safe with the extra stability contributed by the additional crossbands. Burls, crotches, and other woods with irregular or prominently wavy

10-3. Flakeboard core and poplar crossband make most stable 5-ply panel for crotch or burl

grain are quite apt to develop blisters and splits regardless of the kind of core you have used unless they are underlaid with crossband. (10-3)

Second, if you have used fir plywood as a core, you must cover its uneven surface with crossband, or the face veneer will assume the bumpy contour of fir. When you crossband one side, you must crossband the other side to maintain balanced construction. (10-4)

When building 5-ply panels, follow the same technique of turning each sheet to place the grain at right angles to its neighbor.

Thinnest 5-ply panels. There are numerous other combinations you can use in building stable 5-ply panels, lighter in weight, much thinner, but somewhat restricted in their uses. For example, make a core of 3 sheets of 1/20 crossband, crisscrossed method. Face this core with 1/28 choice veneer on one side and 1/28 plain mahogany, sycamore, or poplar on the back. This style of panel can be larger than 3-ply construction because it is stronger and more stable, but it is normally used only in craftwork or as framed paneling for cabinets or chests. It is not strong enough for independent use as a table top or other working surface.

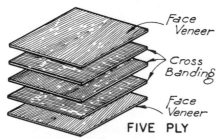

10-2. Here is one way to make a lightweight crisscross panel. Build it of 5 layers of thin veneer

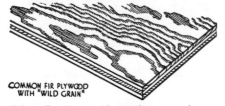

10-4. When fir plywood is used as core, lay crossband over fir, front and back

Solid lumber core. Commercially this is the most expensive grade of plywood. In the home shop it is the most work. (10-5) If you could glue up a few wide boards and use the assembly as a core for veneering, the job would be easy. However, the wider the board the more likely it is to warp. When you cut a wide board into smaller widths, you greatly diminish its warp tendency. The intolerable shrinkage of the 5-inch board in the earlier example is easily avoided. Cut ¾-inch boards into 1½ or 2½ inch widths and turn every other board upside down. This method pits one board against its neighbor. One has a tendency to cup upward; the next wants to cup

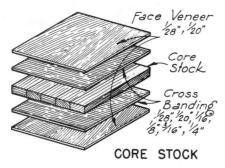

Face Veneer
½8", ½0"

Core
Stock

Cross
Banding
½8", ½0", ½6",
⅛", ³⁄16", ¼"

CORE STOCK

10-5. Five-ply solid lumber core construction is the most work, but provides best edge for finish

downward. They cancel each other out and remain stable. As a practical procedure number each strip as it comes from the circular saw. Turn over every other strip. Letter all edges: right edge of No. 1 strip, A; left edge of No. 2 strip, also A; right edge of No. 2 strip, B. When gluing, A-A edges join, B-B edges, and so on. While you are gluing up 6 or 8 boards you have little time for other details.

The biggest problem of a solid lumber core is planing to assure a level assembly. Planing can best be accomplished on two boards at a time. Clamp them in a bench vise with lettered edges up. Plane smooth and try the joint by placing one edge against the other. The ends should fit tightly, but it is alright if there is a fine opening in the center, because the clamps will draw the boards together and that will make the ends even tighter. If the ends do not fit tightly, the joints will open up after gluing. When you glue up, test the surface for flatness with a steel square. Bring the surface into alignment by striking high

boards with a mallet. When the glued assembly comes out of bar clamps, it usually requires more planing to assure a perfectly flat surface for veneering.

Crossband on core. Always lay crossband of at least 1/20 poplar or equivalent on both sides of the lumber core at right angles to core grain. Crossband evens off the surface and further reduces any warp tendency of the glued-up core. Afterward, lay face veneer on one side at right angles to the crossband; back veneer on the other side, at right angles to the crossband, to complete the veneered panel.

Advantages of solid core. Admittedly there is a great deal of woodworking in construction of a solid core. Why use it? The chief advantage is that it provides the best of all edges for further woodwork and finishing, better than ply criss-cross and better than flakeboard. Solid core presents the best edge appearance. Very often the edge boards of solid core are made of the same wood as the face veneer, or close to it. Core edges can be molded successfully with scratch beader or power shaper. If no woodwork is done to core edges, they still have the advantage of finishing better than other types of panel edges.

Simplest panel, flakeboard core. If weight of a completed panel is of little importance, one of the best and easiest cores to use is the new flakeboard, known also as chipboard and particle board. Flakeboard comes in a variety of thicknesses readily available: ⅜, ½, ⅝, and ¾. This panel board is made of compressed wood chips, resin-impregnated. When buying it for veneering, be sure to buy 45-lb. test or heavier. Edges of the panels are stamped for your verification of test rating. Flakeboard is the most stable of core stock; that is, it is the most warp-free. However, it is the heaviest. It would be unnecessarily heavy for swinging doors of cabinets, and the edges have low holding power for screws. Edges are easily covered with veneer trim. It is ideal for table tops, desk tops, counters, and other working surfaces. Good for sliding doors, headboards, cabinet backs where structural strength is needed for attaching open shelves, and suited to innumerable other purposes.

Because flakeboard is extremely stable, you can use it as a single core for most of your small

10-6. Three-ply construction with flakeboard core is safe for small panels if face veneer is stable

10-7. Hardboard core is safe core for small 3 ply panels. Poplar crossband and butternut face

panels, up to about 18x18. (10-6) Lay face veneer directly on one side, straight-grained veneer of equal thickness on the back, parallel to face grain. Never omit back veneer. Even flakeboard can become distorted by the strong pulling power of one-sided veneering. Back veneer is essential to neutralize the face.

When you build a simple 3-ply panel as just described, you have produced a stable panel. However, there are situations in which you must add crossband, making a 5-ply panel. Crossband in this case is not needed as a stabilizer of the core, but as a stabilizer of the face veneer.

As mentioned constantly for other types of panels, here, too, when you lay crossband under the face you must also lay it under the backing veneer. All brittle face veneers, such as burls, crotches, butts, swirls, bird's-eye, and predominantly wavy grain veneers must be underlaid with crossband or these veneer faces will blister and split. (10-3)

Small panels, hardboard core. Craftwork panels for marquetry pictures, veneer cutouts, and other requirements up to about one square foot in size, can be built with a core of ¼ hardboard, preferably tempered type but not necessarily. (10-7) This core was common practice for

years, but flakeboard is now replacing hardboard where the extra thickness of ⅜ flakeboard can be tolerated.

Hollow-core panels. There are types of woodworking construction which would be awkward, and often impractical, if only solidcore panels could be veneered. For instance, the large swinging door of a cabinet or armoire would be unnecessarily heavy on its hinges if a solid panel were to be used. The shelving members of room dividers, bookshelves attached directly to walls, cabinets and tables that require periodic moving—all such construction would be heavy if solid cores were used.

In most instances it is more practical to substitute hollow-core construction. Briefly, you first make a framework of solid wood. Cover this frame on both sides with thin plywood. Lay veneer over the plywood. It may be more work, but in some cases is almost an essential. Inexpensive ⅛ poplar crossband is a good choice for covering the framework. Several methods of constructing the frame are illustrated. (10-8)

Curved hollow-core. Framework construction is also one of the easiest ways to make curved cabinet doors. Horizontal frame members, in this case, are bandsawed to fit a full-size

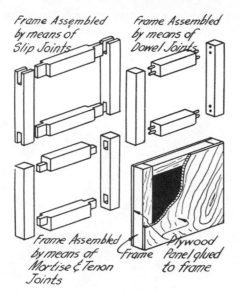

Frame Assembled by means of Slip Joints

Frame Assembled by means of Dowel Joints

Frame Assembled by means of Mortise & Tenon Joints

Frame Plywood Panel glued to frame

10-8. Three ways to make framework for hollow-core panels, useful where light weight is essential

layout of required curvature. Poplar crossband for the covering material, ahead of veneer, will tolerate dry bending if you clamp on, as cauls, the curved pieces left over from bandsawing. Further details are given in chapter 12.

Hollow-core framework construction just described is suited to work which requires special sizes of panels. Where size is not critical, consider the simplified method to follow.

Use doors for cores. The modern style of interior door is a readymade hollow-core framework. It is virtually warp-proof. Some of the discarded doors you pick up cheaply are ready for veneering, with perhaps a small amount of

cleaning up, filling dents and sanding. If you can find only oldstyle fielded-panel doors, these require covering on one side with ¼-inch plywood before you can lay the veneer. Don't use fir for this purpose. Its surface is not smooth enough for direct veneering.

Old doors, when covered on one side with beautiful veneer, make excellent large tables. Standard length for hollow-core doors is 6 ft., 8 in. Widths range from 16 to 30. If the length is oversize for your requirement, cut it down. Cover the open end with a strip of ¼ or ½ wood. Veneer one face and all edges. Screw-fasten a ¾ batten underneath near each end for secure attachment of readymade legs. First, locate the position of cross members of the core frame for attaching the battens. Tap the panel until you locate the solid sound of a cross member.

Choosing the appropriate panel. A wide choice of practical panel construction methods has been described. Usage, of course, should be the prime consideration for the system you select for each piece of work.

Advantages and disadvantages must be taken into account. Stability, weight, size, durability under usage conditions, type of edge needed, finishing characteristics of edges, and availability of materials are the important factors to weigh. Then you have the question, "do I have the tools and equipment, or can I provide essential equipment to perform the work?" Wherever possible, methods developed here have been based on simplified clamping techniques because clamping invariably places the biggest demands on the veneer craftsman.

11. Edge treatments for veneered panels

Veneering panel edges. In furniture construction where the edges of panels are in view, veneered edges present a more artistic appearance than shaped core edges. You would seldom veneer the edge of a panel of less than ½ inch because thinner panels would be framed. Veneering an edge of ½ inch or more is not difficult. In fact, if you follow the modern, simplified method, the work is far easier than ever before.

Using flexible wood trim. This material has taken a lot of work away from edge-veneering. It comes in rolls 8 feet long. Two widths are sold: 1-inch and 2-inch. This is real wood veneer. Don't substitute plastic trim; it cheapens a fine veneered panel. Wood trim is available in mahogany, walnut, teak, oak, birch and Korina which is nearest to white. Using ready-made wood trim is the first work-saver. The next is using the fastest glue.

Using contact glue. If you prefer to use any glue other than contact type you must provide a setup for clamping panel edges. This setup calls for bar clamps and can get fairly complicated. Contact glue is much easier.

Apply wood trim just as it comes from the roll, except for taking the curl out of it by pulling it over a smooth edge, face side against the straightener, as illustrated. (11-1) Cut a length about 1 inch longer than the panel edge you are going to cover.

Brush contact glue on the underside of the wood trim and set it aside for at least 20 minutes to lose its tacky touch. Brush glue on the panel edge and let it stand. Apply contact glue evenly. Get complete coverage, but don't dab with the brush to touch up poorly covered spots while still wet and tacky. Wait until the tack has gone; then spread more glue and let it stand 20 minutes.

To apply the wood trim, lay a slipsheet of wax paper over the panel edge and align one edge of wood trim to one edge of the panel. Let the two glued surfaces touch. If perfectly aligned, press down at the contact edge. (11-2) Pull the slipsheet along slowly and continue to press wood trim to panel edge, always at the aligning edge first. After trim is applied roller it hard. (11-3) This system leaves all of the overhang wood trim along one edge and makes trimming quite easy. It also often gives you a usable leftover strip of wood trim for another piece of work. Store the leftover strip on wax paper to avoid dirt and damage to the glued surface.

Using matching veneer. If you want a perfect match between the edge and a fancy face veneer,

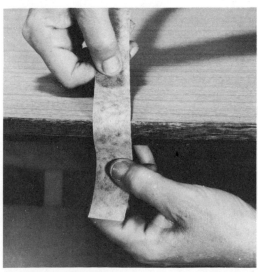

11-1. Take the curl out of wood trim by flexing it over a smooth edge, veneer side against edge

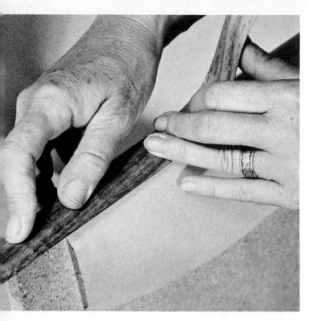

11-2. Apply edging with contact glue. Pull slip-sheet gradually as you perfect the alignment

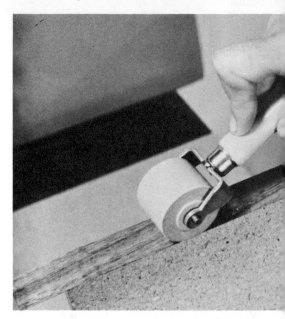

11-3. Roller wood trim hard against edge to assure complete contact. Don't break overhang

you normally will have two choices: cut strips with parallel grain or cross grain. If you elect the somewhat higher-class effect of cross grain, you will have to tape the pieces together to make a long enough strip, because veneer sheets are shorter in cross grain width than in long grain.

11-4. Cut off overhanging edge of wood trim with sharp craft knife. Strip of trim is still usable

You also have two choices of glue for attaching the edging strips. Contact glue can be used without clamps. Squeeze-bottle glues require bar clamps, with protective caul strips the length of the panel. For best gluing results it is well to size end wood with a weak mix of thinned glue and let it dry before applying the regular glue mixture. The prime coat closes open pores in end wood and provides a better bond for the second coat.

The order of applying veneer edging, not wood trim because it is too thin to make much difference, is dependent upon usage of the panel. One safe rule to follow is to apply last the edge seen most. The reason is that the last piece put in place will cover the ends of earlier pieces.

It is good policy to trim each overhang as soon as the glue has set, instead of waiting to trim all four edges at one time. You run less risk of snapping off the overhang by getting it off as soon as possible. Place the veneered edge, face down, on a smooth workboard. Trim with a craft knife, working from end toward center, never outward across an end. (11-4) Sand the edge gently in the same direction. This is the safe way to prevent splitting the veneer trim.

Shaping edges. It is possible to lay the super-thin 1/64 veneer on curved edges of simple de-

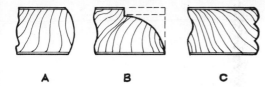

| A | B | C |

11-5. Shaping edge of core panel by hand. **A.** Gauge a pencil line on each face, about 3/16 from edge. Use spokeshave to work out rough rounded shape. Smooth with cabinet scraper and sandpaper. **B.** First cut or plane a rabbet, shown by dotted lines. Next, round the edge with block plane. Protect veneer from plane damage by clamping scrap stock along the veneer edge. Cut cardboard template to check shape constantly. **C.** Beaded edge is literally scraped into wood by many passes with scratch beader

sign. Half-round and quarter-round edges can be veneered as a final operation before finishing. It simply is not practical to lay standard veneers on fancier, shaped edges.

If you want a molded edge on a veneered panel, a solid-core panel is the most practical kind to make. You can shape a simple edge by hand with a plane and spokeshave, and then smooth it with cabinet scraper and sandpaper. (11-5) You can get a little fancier with a molding plane or a homemade scratch beader, which is a hand-size piece of wood fitted with a piece of hacksaw blade or 1/16 steel ground to desired shape. (*See* Tricks of Trade.) Of course a power shaper provides the best and cleanest way to cut an intricate molding around your veneered panel.

Concealing plywood edges. If your veneered panel has been built of crossbands and veneers instead of a solid core, neither hand nor power shaping is practical. Assuming that you are looking for a treatment other than the obvious one of gluing veneer to the edge, you will find quite a variety of treatments in standard use.

Many shapes of molding are offered by local lumberyards. Several types illustrated are the most popular because they do not detract from a beautifully veneered panel. (11-6) Edging should be finished and mitered before it is attached to the panel edge with glue. Brads are completely unnecessary and unsightly.

Variations can be worked out by using a molding just slightly narrower than the edge. It is applied flush with the bottom edge of the panel but dropped down from the face edge enough to utilize the veneer edge as part of the molded design. (11-7)

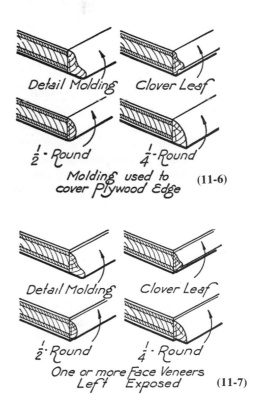

Detail Molding   Clover Leaf

$\frac{1}{2}$-Round $\frac{1}{4}$-Round

Molding used to cover Plywood Edge   (11-6)

Detail Molding   Clover Leaf

$\frac{1}{2}$-Round $\frac{1}{4}$-Round

One or more Face Veneers Left Exposed   (11-7)

12. Veneering curved panels

It is easier to veneer curved work than it used to be. Before introduction of contact instant-set glue elaborate setups with curved cauls and sometimes sand boxes were commonplace. These methods will be explained here, but they should be your last choice for veneering curved panels. Where you have the option, use the contact glue system.

Pre-curved panels. Only the panels which have been curved to desired shape can be veneered with contact glue. One such type is the curved door front of a cabinet or the drawer front of a chest or table. Many period pieces of furniture have this style of door and may now need new veneer. If the old veneer is broken, blistered or in any way unsound, remove it by any appropriate means. You can try heating the old glue with a hot iron. You can pry some of the veneer off with a chisel, and remove the rest by power sanding.

Another type of curved panel of course is the one you make by accurately bandsawing a thick block of wood to the desired shape. This type, also, is fairly easy to veneer with contact glue: first the back, or inside, then the edges and finally the face.

Bending veneer on pre-curved panel. If for some structural reason you wish to veneer a curved panel with regular liquid glue, you need cauls. (12-1) While bandsawing the curved piece, you create a top and a bottom caul. Save these and use them to force the flat sheets of veneer, front and back, to take the shape of the core. Glue and press in the same way next described for the sand-box curving method.

Bending in a sand box. If the curved work is a piece you have not bandsawed, you have no cauls. In this case try the sand box method.

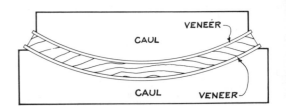

12-1. Above, curved core being veneered on two sides. Bandsawed top and bottom cauls conform to shape of core. At least two sets of cauls are needed. Below, curving panel without a core requires two sets of cauls. Handscrews apply gradual pressure. Useful system for one to three sheets of veneer

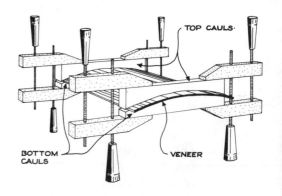

12-2. Irregular shapes are sometimes formed in a sand box. Method requires a shaped caul or core

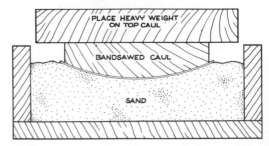

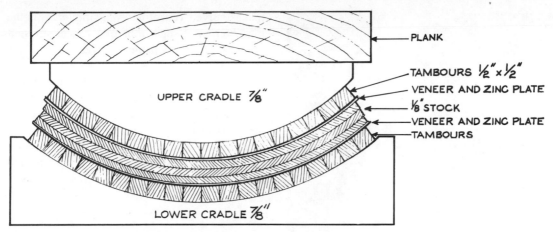

12-3. Making large, stable, curved-panel doors is complicated task for the home-shop craftsman

(12-2) Fill a non-porous cloth bag with fine, sifted sand. Place it in a strong box. Force the sand bag into shape by pressing hard and evenly with the curved core. Remove the core, apply glue, lay the veneer on the glued surface and return the assembly to the sand box. Weight the core heavily but gradually, preferably in a veneer press. Increase pressure before the glue has really begun to set.

If sand is objectionable, cast a bottom caul of plaster of Paris into which excelsior has been mixed for extra strength.

Forming curved cabinet doors. The most involved method of creating a curved door, too wide to bandsaw, is a core arrangement that is curved at the same time as crossbands. (12-3)

First the core and crossbands are glued and bent. Front and back veneers are then glued to the core and returned to the press.

The first thing is to determine the thickness of the door and amount of curvature. Make a full-size drawing of this cross section, including squared sticks, called tambours, and cradles.

Two cradles are always needed; that is, two top and two bottom cradles. If the door is long, make three cradles and space them on dowels about 8 inches apart.

Tambours are made of ½ stock a little longer than the door. They are held loosely together with cord passed through holes bored in them. In this way they adjust themselves to any curvature.

The core is composed of 3 or 4 layers of ⅛ single-ply poplar. These are placed together. Inside and outside surfaces are covered with 1/20 crossbanding, turned at right angles to the core on which they will be glued.

Place crossbanding together, spread quickly with glue on all sides. Drive a nail at each end of the pile. Do not add back and face veneers at this time. Lay a thin metal sheet or thin hardboard on both sides of the glued-up work. Put in the press between cradles. Lay a few sheets of flat newspaper on the veneer. It is most important to center the work accurately. Do this by drawing centerlines for alignment. Apply pressure gradually. The filler sheet of metal or hardboard prevents the wood from cracking as it is being bent under pressure.

When removed from the press, the assembly is trimmed at both ends, and a piece of ½ stock glued to both edges, smoothed flush with both surfaces. Now the assembly is ready to be returned to the cauls with front and back veneers glued in place. For a finished appearance and convenience in hinging, glue solid strips of wood to the edges.

Covering curved shapes with flexible veneer. The foregoing methods for veneering curved pieces were based on the customary use of standard veneer thicknesses of 1/28 and 1/40. Contact glue provided the simplest method. Now another advance in the veneer industry

makes curved veneering even simpler. It is the introduction of super-thin 1/64 veneer sheets 8 feet long. (12-4) Chapter 4 gives more details about availability.

Flexible veneer is real wood laminated to a flexible backing which is not removable. It tolerates a lot of bending, even over rounded corners. Contact glue again provides the best adhesive for use on flexible veneer, if for no other reason than the impractical use of clamps and cauls on rounded or extra-large flat surfaces.

12-4. Bow-front drawer from drum table being upgraded with new face veneer. This is super-thin rosewood, flexible, tolerant of bending. Photograph shows trial fitting before contact glue is spread on both surfaces. Closest edge will be the aligning edge. Back edge overhangs for trimming. Notice that veneer grain runs vertically as it should in good cabinetwork

13. Removing tape, trimming, sanding, finishing

Preparing veneered surfaces for finishing sometimes requires several operations; other times, just light sanding. Because of these differences in the condition of completed work, some of the steps detailed here will apply only part of the time.

Cleaning off tape. Where you have only a strip or two of gum tape covering a split or a matched joint, removal of the tape is quite easy. Where you have an entire face covered with tape, such as the fraternal emblems and the chess board veneer faces shown in chapter 2 you must allow more time and patience. It takes both.

For moistening the tape, use a cellulose sponge that has no soap or abrasive additives. For picking it up, use a thin-bladed stick-shellac spatula, or locate the thinnest, flattest, bluntest knife in the kitchen. Other standard equipment is illustrated in chapter 5.

Moisten the tape with water. With the recommended sponge, the most manageable water applicator, you can put moisture on the tape without getting the surrounding wood wet. Work on no more than about 4 square inches at a time. Wait a few moments for penetration, then pick up a corner of tape with the blunt knife and peel slowly. (13-1) If it resists completely, more sponging. Single strips of tape will come off readily. Large, sometimes crisscrossed areas respond very little to a first gentle attempt. Soon, however, you will peel off a first layer. The tape actually splits apart and leaves a second fuzzy layer, much harder to remove. Moisten this layer less than the first. You are nearer to the wood. Peel anything that sticks up. Avoid the temptation to soak it and get it over with. You will not only damage the wood, but also loosen the glue bond beneath it. Take it easy.

A sharp chisel (13-2) held like a scraper, almost straight up, and pulled toward you, can help immeasurably in loosening the stubborn areas that are too fragmented to get hold of to peel. Another tool, the cabinet scraper, (13-3) can go to work on the final cleanup. Hold it angled toward you and pull it toward you while pressing down. When used carefully neither chisel nor scraper will gouge the wood. If all you have is the popular handled type of scraper,

13-1. To remove paper tape from a split or joint, moisten lightly with sponge, lift with spatula

13-2. After peeling paper tape from joint, scrape joint with straight chisel to remove gum residue

13-3. Cabinet scraper is best tool for final cleanup of gum and scratches. Brazilian rosewood panel

(13-4) round the ends slightly with a file; otherwise they leave permanent scratches.

Almost any moistening required for tape removal is dangerous. It is best to place the work back in clamps or under heavy weight for overnight.

First, check for dents and nicks in the surface. Use an eyedropper to spot drops of hot water on such depressions. In most cases the wood cells will absorb enough water to swell back to their normal surface.

If veneer pins are still present, remove or sink them below the surface and fill the tiny pinholes with melted stick shellac. Spots of grease inadvertently dropped can be removed with naphtha.

Trimming overhang. Some trimming must be done during construction. Final trimming can be done at this stage. It depends on your project. Panels, for instance, exhibit cleaner edges if you veneer one side at a time. Take a panel from clamps and trim the overhang at once before it gets chipped from handling. (13-5)

Gluing veneer to both sides of a panel in one operation and trying to trim the double overhang afterwards, as often advocated, seems unnecessarily difficult. If time is the reason for doubling

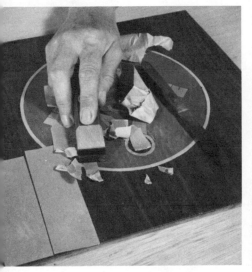

13-4. Handled scraper can be used to remove paper tape if corners are filed to prevent scratching

13-5. Trim veneer overhang from first veneered side before laying veneer face on opposite side

up, consider the fact that modern glues allow the safe removal of work from clamps within 3 to 4 hours, possibly sooner, at which time the first overhang can be trimmed and the second side veneered.

Tape reduces chipping. When cutting overhang, especially cross-grain which chips more readily than long grain, for extra security lay clear tape on the underside along the cut line. (13-6) It does not completely stop chipping, but it reduces it.

Sanding panel edges. Trimmed edges always need sanding. Usually they can be sanded very lightly with a sanding block held at an angle. (13-7) This technique avoids all possibility of having the edge of sandpaper pick up an imperceptible sliver and rip it into a major defect. Occasionally a trimmed edge will require heavier sanding where the strong grain of the veneer face pulled your knife away from the panel edge.

The problem to guard against when sanding edges is chipping the face veneer. Favor the face veneer by pushing the sanding block away from veneer edge; always pushing, never pulling it across the edge.

13-6. Clear tape laid on underside of overhang, before trimming, reduces chipping of cross grain

13-7. Fine sandpaper, 220, on block held at angle to prevent edge of paper from picking up splinter

13-8. Power sander fitted with fine, used sandpaper can be used only briefly to clean marquetry

Power sanding. (13-8) Using a power sander on veneer can be dangerous unless you take extra precaution. Before you know it, the machine could cut through at the edge, especially if the veneer is only 1/40 thick.

Here are several precautions to observe: equip the machine with the finest possible sandpaper, preferably a used sheet; hold it off the work when starting the motor; keep the machine moving; don't run out across an edge; keep at least ⅔ of the sanding platten on the face when ⅓ is outboard at the edge.

Don't power sand to remove tape and glue residue. Manufactured wood products which have been faced with marquetry veneer—such as chess boards, fancy boxes, plaques and other so-called "inlaid" pieces—have been cleaned of gum tape by an industrial sander.

The sanding equipment you have is not adequate for that method. In fact, if you apply your power sanding tools to the tape, the friction generated will tend to soften the glue and make it stick even harder when it cools. Apply your power sander only after all residue of tape and glue has been cleaned off by the methods detailed earlier.

Brush off sanding grit. Keep a hand-size, moderately stiff-bristled brush within reach. Use it frequently to sweep sanding dust and grit from work in progress. (13-9) Stop sanding to clean the work; otherwise you inevitably scratch the veneer. Use this brush to sweep your workboard, too. Keep it free of sanding grit, chips and shards of veneer. This is an important discipline to develop.

WOOD FINISHING

Wood finishing materials have changed substantially in recent years. Finishing techniques are gradually changing to make the most of the improved, modern materials. Many craftsmen are slow to discard their conventional methods, and will now want to carry them into the area of

13-9. Clean sanding grit from wood pores with scrub brush. Tap brush often to shake out grit

veneer finishing. Finishing is admittedly a subject of broad differences among amateurs as well as professionals.

For these reasons, and because the subject of modern wood finishing is too detailed to cover dependably in limited space, only a brief philosophy about finishing will follow. The work you have accomplished in veneering is too precious to complete with anything but the very best finish you can apply. Your most reliable guidance on modern methods is expertly related in the new book by Michael DeMeo, entitled *Step-by-step Pro Finishing for the Amateur*.

Some woods are so naturally beautiful that in the opinion of some woodworkers no stain at all should be applied. If this is your view, and if the wood has closed pores, you can spray on two or three light coats of polyurethane varnish if the work is small. (13-10) The aerosol unit illustrated attaches to a jar in which varnish is poured. Just follow the general rules for spraying: start the spray outboard, not in front of the work; move it at an even pace straight across the work, never in an arc; apply only a light coat at a time; rub down evenly when dry with fine steel wool; apply several light coats in the same way.

For larger work you can apply the same type of varnish with a finishing brush. (13-11) Polyurethane varnish creates a satin-smooth protective finish, entirely appropriate to color veneers. In fact, it actually intensifies and enriches the natural color of the wood.

You can apply much lighter coats with the spray unit than you can with a brush. For spraying, prop up the work as nearly vertical as possible without having it fall forward. Never use the

spray unit pointing down. For this reason you cannot spray large panels. They must be brushed. Never brush veneer-craft cutouts which have been overlaid on a panel. Veneer edges will cause the finish to pile up and you will not be able to clean it off. Never attempt to rub down with steel wool any type of overlay design.

Woods like plain mahogany and maple develop their characteristic coloring very slowly, and for this reason they usually are color-enriched with stain. Open-pore woods like mahogany, walnut, oak, lacewood, burls and others need an application of wood filler for enrichment. Filler follows stain, and filler should be of matching color. Final coats are largely a matter of personal preference for high-gloss, satin or dull finishes. They are created with polyurethane varnish, or other varnishes or lacquers, followed by rubbing down with fine abrasive powders, pumice and rottenstone.

Burls need filler. If you hold a sheet of burl veneer up to the light, you will see pinholes. Some burls, olive ash for instance, may have

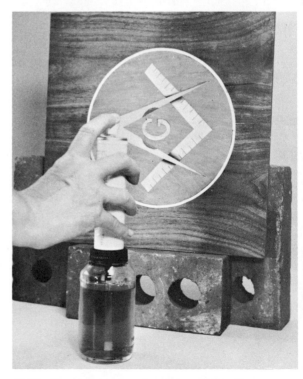

13-10. Support veneered panel upright. Spray two very light coats of clear urethane varnish

13-11. Clear urethane varnish is brushed on panel of rosewood. Brushing lays heavier coat

pinholes in such profusion you will wonder if the sheet you are inspecting will be satisfactory. It will, if you fill it.

Use natural silex wood filler on light woods. For dark woods you can tint natural filler sparingly with Japan colors. Apply filler to the veneer according to instructions on the can. Usually this means mixing a small amount in naphtha to get a creamy consistency. Apply to the veneer. Allow about 10 minutes to dry. Wipe off excess filler with a piece of burlap, wiping across grain so that the filler remains packed in the pores of the wood. Wait 24 hours, preferably

more, before you apply clear finish of your choice.

What happens if you skip filler? Most burls will split and blister in pinhole areas after you have glued the veneer to the panel. The reason is this: the vehicle of the finish material, that is, the turpentine or thinner, will sink through the pinholes and dissolve glue under the veneer. You have caused a veneering failure which normally defies correction. To avoid this unacceptable situation, always spread filler on burls in which you have seen pinholes when holding the piece up to the light.

14. How to repair veneering defects

After a veneered panel has been cleaned of gum paper, glue spots, and marks acquired during processing, it should be inspected for construction faults. At this stage it still may require further work before you apply any form of wood finish.

Make a careful inspection for areas which you think you can improve. Look for edge lifting. Inspect all joints where veneers have been jointed. Examine for splits. Feel for blisters. These construction faults are more easily repaired on raw wood. The time to patch and fill is now.

Edge lifting. This is a common fault having any of several causes. The panel you veneered could have been slightly undercut at the edge when you veneered it. This condition comes most often from over-sanding along edges. The second cause, in order of frequency, is inadequate clamping at the edge. The top caul could

have been too thin for the size of panel being veneered. The caul could have bowed under pressure. It could have been warped when you used it. You could have applied too much clamp pressure with clamps that were too far apart. The third common cause of edge lifting is poor glue coverage at the edge. Possible causes are pointed out here so that future work can be watched more carefully. The immediate problem of edge lifting is easy to correct.

If the panel is of manageable size, support it in an upright position with the offending edge upward. One of the simplest setups for securely supporting an upright panel is illustrated as a practical work holder in chapter 15.

For this repair, liquid white glue is preferred, regardless of what you used for gluing the panel. You cannot use contact glue now. White glue flows best and is easiest to work into the crack.

Work glue into the opening between veneer

14-1. Edge lifting is repaired by using spatula to carry white glue into crack. Have panel vertical

14-2. Clamp heavy bearer blocks front and back of repaired edge. Glue squeeze-out comes off

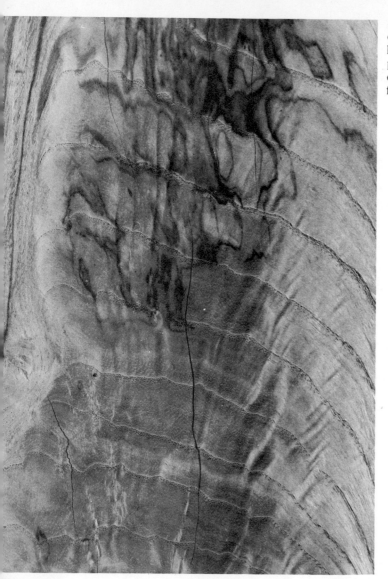

14-3. Cracks developed in this aspen crotch because no crossband was laid under the face veneer. This was purposeful to prove importance of crossband and to provide a cracked face in need of repair

and panel. Use a very thin spatula or the blade of your craft knife. (14-1) Do not use a scrap of veneer. It is too thick and it could break off inside the crack. Spatula and knife are thin enough to carry glue into the crack. The illustrated small spatula is the best instrument. It causes no damage to the veneer. By having the panel upright you are getting a lot of help from gravity. White glue flows deep into the crack.

If the condition of edge lifting was caused by an undercut panel, white glue alone will not accomplish a satisfactory repair. The crack needs filling. Mix fine sawdust, made from matching wood, with white glue and use it as a filler. Pack filler into the crack with the spatula. Allow about 5 minutes or so for it to start setting before you apply clamps. Clamps will squeeze out the excess filler. It will scrape off when dry.

Place heavy bearer blocks on both sides of the panel. Place a piece of wax paper between block and veneer. (14-2) Bearer blocks distribute pressure along the edge. In about 30 minutes pick off as much glue squeeze-out as you can reach without disturbing the setup in any way.

Concealing cracks. When unruly fancy veneers are properly laid on crossband they seldom develop noticeable cracks. As a negative experiment to see just how important this crossbanding principle really is, two choice pieces of fancy veneer were laid on stable flakeboard panels without crossband beneath. The panels did not warp, demonstrating that flakeboard is a very stable material to use as a core. However, both veneers used in the experiment developed conspicuous cracks in a very short time. These experimental panels, one aspen crotch, the other thuya burl, serve as dual lessons in veneering. First, never lay veneers of this type without crossband. Second, how to conceal cracks in veneer, whatever the cause may have been.

In the aspen crotch panel (14-3) a long, straight crack developed up the middle of the figure. Smaller cracks continued to appear. They required filling. In this demonstration the techniques of filling with stick shellac are shown.

Stick shellac is just what its name implies. It is a bar of hardened shellac compound about the size of a heavy pencil. It comes in a variety of shades ranging from the color of light oak to red and brown mahogany, light and dark walnut, cherry, ebony, holly, maple, and transparent. This selection enables you to come very close to matching the wood you are filling. When two shades of shellac are close, choose the lighter.

Shellac becomes sufficiently molten and tacky when rubbed with a hot spatula so that it can be scraped onto the wood. (14-4) By reheating the spatula quickly you still have time to press the shellac into the crack. Build it up a little above wood surface and feather the edges. It rehardens fast when it cools. This characteristic makes it an ideal wood filler for concealment of veneer cracks.

Heating the spatula over a small alcohol lamp is standard practice. If you are confronted with an immediate need to fill a crack and do not own an alcohol lamp, you can use a makeshift. Pour a few tablespoons of alcohol solvent in a small tin can. Place a lamp wick or a twist of cotton cord in the can. Light the wick and hold your spatula over the flame. If your improvised wick goes out

too often, light the alcohol in the bottom of the can. There is not enough to create fire danger. If you have nothing but canned heat or the kitchen gas stove for a flame source, your spatula will gather soot. Before touching shellac, wipe the hot blade with medium steel wool and then with

14-4. Stick shellac, matching aspen color, heated by spatula, fills crack. Alcohol in can heats tool

14-5. Stick shellac, mounded over crack, hardens as it cools. Clean up with chisel and sandpaper

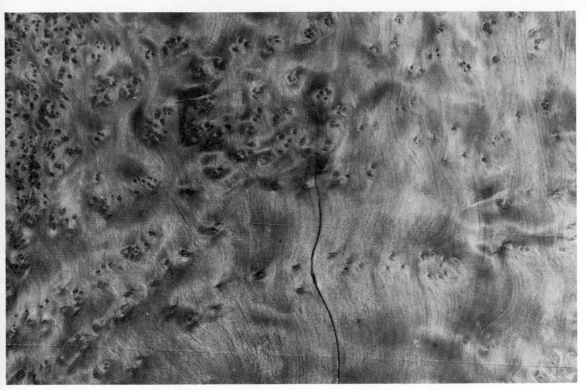

14-6. Another method for repairing cracked veneer. Thuya burl was laid without crossband under it to prove value of crossband and provide a predictable cracked panel for repair demonstration

a clean cloth to remove the soot. The tin-can system is less trouble.

Allow overnight for hardening of the shellac repair. Use a chisel for cleanup. (14-5) Scrape down the mounded shellac and scrape away the inevitable spots created when you feathered the edges with the spatula. Fortunately you are working on raw wood and are not concerned with damaging a fine wood finish. This proves the importance of careful inspection and repair before you apply finish of any kind to veneer. Repairs to finished furniture involve problems that are beyond the scope of this book on veneering construction. Just incidentally, a tip coming from a wood finishing expert is added. Satin, low-gloss finishes are best for concealing tiny, hairline checking. That is, checks are more noticeable under high-gloss finishes.

In the thuya burl experimental panel, laid without crossband in violation of good practice, a wide, curving crack appeared, following the swirling grain. (14-6) In this demonstration the crack will be repaired by another technique. When a wood is hard to match with a standard stick-shellac color, use sawdust from the same wood to fill the crack.

To produce matching sawdust locate a scrap of leftover veneer of the same kind as the panel face. Use your small saw to scrape sawdust onto wax paper. (14-7) Avoid sandpaper for this job. Cut a strip of scrap veneer for a spatula. Make a separate mound of white glue. Pick up a tiny amount of glue on the spatula and dab the stick in the sawdust. You want just a little more glue than sawdust to start. Scrape the mix across the crack. (14-8) Next, pick up less glue and more sawdust so that sawdust predominates at the top of the crack. Work at the crack without worrying too much about mess around it. Leave the mix somewhat mounded over the crack. Allow overnight to dry. Use your chisel to scrape off excess and to remove slight discoloration where the glue smeared. Sand after scraping. You are working on raw wood, which is much easier to blend than finished wood.

One factor helping concealment in this instance is that the filled crack, without close examination, will appear to be a streak of swirling grain. This principle is one to remember. Wherever you have a choice in making a repair, work with existing grain; parallel the grain as much as possible. Formal, geometric patches and repairs should be totally avoided. If you cannot follow grain pattern, at least make the repair of irregular shape.

Filling joints. Where you have joined two sheets of veneer to cover a panel, usually as back veneer, the joint ordinarily is visible. To conceal it and to stop moisture penetration before you can apply finish, fill the joint. Follow either of the two crack-filling methods described.

Repairing blisters. New work should be kept under full cauls, moderately weighted, until finish can be applied. This practice reduces the effects of humidity changes which can cause blisters.

Humidity is not the only cause of blisters. The most common cause is poor bonding between veneer and panel because of insufficient rollering. The next cause is inadequate glue coverage.

The first remedy to try on a blister in order to lay it flat on the panel is rollering. If the blister is substantial in size and fairly high, rollering must be done with care, first around the edges to test the reaction. If you start rollering in the middle of a large blister you likely will split the veneer.

The next try should be made with heat. If glue coverage was adequate, but contact poor, heat

14-7. To fill crack with matching wood, use saw, not sandpaper, to make sawdust from thuya

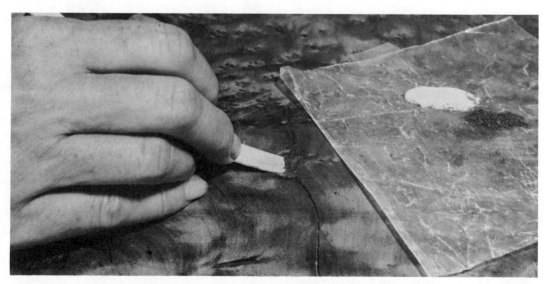

14-8. Make separate mounds of sawdust and white glue. With scrap of veneer for flexible spatula, pick up glue, then sawdust. Scrape across crack. Clean up and sand when dry

14-9. Blisters often can be repaired with hot iron. Softens glue momentarily. Foil protects veneer

14-10. Blisters having no glue underneath require slitting along two edges in direction of grain

will soften the glue. That gives you another chance to provide a good bond with plenty of pressure.

A household electric iron is the best heat source for the purpose. Lay a sheet of aluminum foil over the veneer and work the iron back and forth. (14-9) The iron should be only moderately hot. After a few strokes, lift the iron and roller the blistered area. Repeat the heat and rollering a few times. Be prepared ahead of time to place the treated area in clamps at once. A wood block somewhat larger than the blistered area provides a better way to apply concentrated pressure than the use of a full caul. Work out your clamping arrangement in advance.

A blister caused by inadequate glue must be reglued. A stubborn blister in curly veneer that has warped and will not flatten out should be reglued. In either situation make two slits, one along each edge of the blister, not down the center. The reason for this is that a center slit lets too much glue accumulate in one spot and none at the edges.

Slit the veneer with the grain, not across it. (14-10) Lift the veneer with a knife point until you have enough opening to insert a syringe-like tool called a glue injector. (14-11) Force only a small amount of glue under the veneer. Press the veneer to spread the glue. Repeat the treatment

in the opposite slit. Use the wood block system for applying concentrated pressure. If this blister rises after clamps are removed, go back to the electric iron technique. It has a better chance of working this time, because you have put some glue under the blister.

14-11. Lift veneer with knife point. Force white glue, with injector, under slits toward center

15. Useful tricks of the trade

Making thin veneer thinner. If you make veneer craft cutouts or marquetry pictures, as most craftsmen do at one time or another, you find yourself using two thicknesses of veneer, 1/28 and 1/40. This variation is due to the fact that veneers are no longer of one standard 1/28 thickness.

Adjoining elements of the design should be the same thickness. To overcome the variation, here is a handy trick to know.

Locate a piece of 1/28 that suits your requirement for color and grain. The piece selected should be quite flat and close-grained. Padauk was used in the demonstration. (15-1)

Plane down the 1/28 to the thickness of the adjoining piece in your cutout assembly; that is, to about 1/40. Secure the veneer to a board or square of plywood by driving veneer pins around the edges of the veneer. Sink them very slightly below the surface with a small nail set or a nail ground flat at the point. Now take a few shavings off the surface with a very sharp plane, set extremely fine. Drive the pins deeper and proceed to take off more shavings until the wood matches the thickness of a 1/40 piece laid beside it. You will probably sink a few pins through the veneer and will have to add more as you work.

Substitute for bar clamps. Unless you are a professional cabinetmaker you probably do not own all the clamps you need. Most amateur woodworkers do not own long bar clamps which are thought to be essential when making up core stock for veneered panels. If you are reluctant to make the investment in several bar clamps for your shop, here is a substitute method. (15-2)

You can make a heavy wood frame for a lot less than the cost of clamps for the same purpose. Low-cost rough lumber, even used 2x4's, and about 4 pieces of scrap ¾ x 4 x 30 will make a good gluing frame. Since a 2-foot by 4-foot veneered panel is about the largest size practical for home-shop manufacture, the sidepieces of the frame should measure about 5 feet long, or shorter if you expect to stay within the average 3-foot sheet of veneer.

Attach the 4 crosspieces of ¾ stock with nails or screws to the 2 sidepieces. Fasten crosspieces all on the same side, and make certain of having them strong and rack-free.

Prepare two pairs of wedges from 2x4. Lay the assembled frame across two sawhorses or other flat support. Lay the strips of wood you have cut for core stock on the crosspieces, with strong glue such as Titebond on all edges except the outer edges. Force the wedges into position to tighten the assembly. (15-3)

If the panel you are preparing is considerably narrower than the gluing frame, simply add enough filler strips at the edge opposite to the wedging end. There, they will have no tendency to slip.

15-1. Where you have no choice but to use thick and thin veneer adjoining, plane thick piece

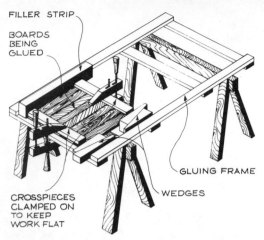

FILLER STRIP

BOARDS
BEING
GLUED

GLUING FRAME

WEDGES

CROSSPIECES
CLAMPED ON
TO KEEP
WORK FLAT

15-2. Clamping frame made of used lumber avoids investment in bar clamps for solid core

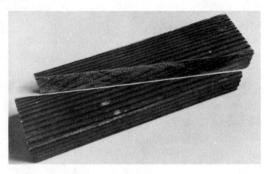

15-3. Wedges are the simple solution to providing pressure in frame without big bar clamps

Heavy bearer strips, such as scrap lengths of 2x4, are next laid across the glued-up panel and underneath the panel in matching locations. Handscrews or C-clamps are drawn up tight to keep the work flat until the glue has set, preferably overnight.

Additional uses for this handy gluing frame will arise. You will need it for gluing edges to panels with any kind of glue except contact type. In furniture construction and furniture repair work it will repay you many times over.

Concealing panel joints. Where you are using your veneered panels as covering for a large surface such as a wall, the major problem is concealment of the panel joint. Two ply panels coming together will inevitably leave a noticeable open joint. Several methods of inconspicuous jointing are practiced. One is to insert batten strips either of matching wood or of intentional contrasting wood. (15-4)

Another method, creating a more subtle joint line, is the flush banding strip. (15-5) To accomplish this concealment, each ply.panel is rabbeted to veneer thickness for a width of ½ inch. This makes an overall rabbet of 1 inch into which a strip of matching veneer edging is glued. One difficulty is the inexact match of the edging with the facing veneer. Another difficulty is the rabbet. Router or rabbet plane can do it if you have the suitable cutters. However, a little-known woodworker's trick is somewhat easier and is the best concealment of all methods. It uses the face veneer of one panel to conceal the joint.

When you are ready to trim the overhang from the panel you have veneered, trim the righthand edge flush. Mark a 3/16 overhang on the left edge and trim on the mark. Now use a purfling cutter, a router or other means to cut a 3/16 wide rabbet on the right edge of each panel. The left overhang fits into the righthand rabbet of the adjoining panel, making as neat a joint as your workmanship can produce. It is virtually invisible especially if you have laid a face veneer with noticeable grain. The thin joint line blends with the grain. One word of warning is timely: a large panel with a 3/16 veneer overhang obviously

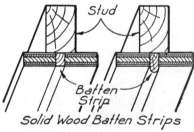

Stud

Batten Strip

Solid Wood Batten Strips

15-4. Panel joints are usually more conspicuous than deliberate separation by solid wood battens

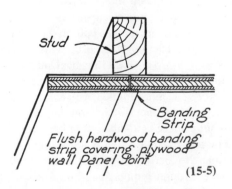

Stud

Banding Strip

Flush hardwood banding strip covering plywood wall Panel Joint

(15-5)

15-6. Two-foot length of angle iron clamped to a table holds panels handily upright for edging

demands extreme care in handling until you secure it to the surface you are paneling.

Practical workholder. This simplified workholder beats many of the elaborate clamping setups craftsmen resort to now and then. (15-6) You need only four C-clamps and a length of angle iron from the junkyard where old bed rails are easily found. It is an ideal system for holding a panel while you are applying edge-veneer. It is quick to set up and wobble-free. If you keep the angle iron handy you will probably use this scheme as a workholder for other types of woodworking jobs, such as planing, filing, carving, assembling, and even repairing window screens.

Test veneer for soft side. Cabinetmakers test a sheet of veneer to determine which side has softest grain and therefore will chip out most readily when the overhang is being trimmed off with a knife. When determined, the soft side is the one to glue down.

All veneers have this characteristic—one soft, one tight side—but the difference is more evident in some woods than in others. Mahogany and walnut, for instance, have a conspicuous soft side. When you know how to find it, you will produce better, cleaner edges. (15-7)

15-7. The way veneer is sliced creates a soft side. Identify by thumb test. Glue the soft side

The soft, or loose grain, side of a veneer sheet may be found by rubbing your finger over the end, intentionally trying to chip it. Try this test on both sides. On one side small chips will break off more readily. This is the soft side. Glue it to the panel.

When you are matching consecutive sheets to create a matched design, this test is meaningless, because every other sheet must be reversed regardless of soft side. There is no choice.

Make a scratch beader. One of the most useful ideas for shaping an attractive edge on panels you have veneered for table tops and chest tops comes from professional wood carvers. Called a scratch beader, it is suited to solid wood edges—solid core, not plywood.

The blade holder is made of two pieces of ½ or ¾ stock, 3 inches wide and 6 inches long. (15-8) Notch each piece as shown. Drill holes to take two bolts for wing nuts. A third hole allows movement of the cutter, mainly for surface cutting instead of edge cutting.

For the blade, you need a piece of steel about 1/32 or 1/16 thick. Width depends on your intended usage. If only narrow molding is to be cut, use an old hacksaw blade. Shape the steel with files, round and three-square. When filing, be sure to keep the edge of the cutter square, not beveled or rounded. Remove the wire edge, left

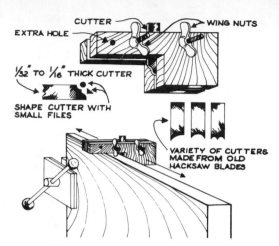

15-8. Homemade scratch beader is hard to beat as an efficient molding tool for solid panel edges

by filing, by rubbing both faces on an oilstone.

This is a scraping beader, not a cutting tool. Always drag it squarely across the edge you are molding. Work it forward and backward. Make many passes with the beader, never too hard, until required depth has been reached.

Test for best light reflection. There are four directions in which you can lay a sheet of face veneer on a core. Side 1 up for face; side 1 turned over for gluing down; side 1 with edge 1 to right; side 1 with edge 1 to left.

15-9. Save time and aggravation by learning to open or tighten handscrews quickly as possible

To determine the most attractive way to lay the face veneer try the light test. Hold the sheet flat if intended for a table top. Hold it vertically if intended as an upright panel. Turning it end for end does not always make sense, but it does count if you are making a table top with a drawer, which of course will face in a prescribed direction.

See how window light or lamp light changes the sheen. You will be amazed at how much more attractive reflected light makes one of the directions. When feasible, make this test in the general location of final usage.

If the light test seems to conflict with the thumb test for soft side, remember that some uses for veneered panels bury the edges in a frame, such as a framed cabinet door or a tray molding. It therefore would not matter where the soft side were used.

Unscramble handscrews. These wood clamps are so essential in veneering that it pays to learn to handle them speedily, as few amateurs do unless they have been taught.

Always pick up a handscrew as shown. (15-9) They rarely have the right opening for the job at hand. The left hand grasps the middle spindle; the right hand grasps the end spindle. Hold the handles firmly and revolve the spindles with a swinging motion. Swinging the jaws inward toward the face will open them; in the other direction, close them. This quickly becomes automatic and saves much time and aggravation when you are hurrying to apply them.

In placing a handscrew on the work, put the left hand underneath, the right hand above. On vertical work put the right hand to the right. These correct positions always leave the right hand ready to tighten the jaws last.

Place the handscrew so that the middle spindle is as close to the work as possible. Then adjust one or both spindles so that the handscrew grips the edge of the work easily while the point of the jaws remains slightly open. The middle spindle ordinarily requires no further adjustment. Tighten the jaws now by turning the end spindle until the work is gripped uniformly, that is, with flat jaws.

To be sure the pressure is even, try moving the jaws from side to side. If they do move, tighten the end spindle still more.

15-10. Protect veneered face from scratches by holding your improvised straightedge as shown

Dyeing veneers. A curiosity about dyeing methods has intrigued most craftsmen who have used dyed woods. It seems that each person wants a very special color. Dyeing in the home shop is messy, very limited in color range, and of doubtful outcome. Nevertheless the effort still persists. With thanks to George R. Bordewick who has solved many of the problems this abbreviated report is passed along.

Add a half-pound of drug-store ferrous sulphate to one gallon of water in a glass vessel. Immerse and leave the veneer in the solution until complete penetration has been accomplished. Remove the wood from solution, wash under a water tap, press between newspaper and caul boards until dry and flat. Change newspaper daily.

Sycamore becomes dark with a pleasing mottle figure; red gumwood turns black; oak, kelobra and butternut turn almost purple.

Trim overhang long. Veneered panels are normally trimmed flush with a craft knife. When you trim overhang on boxes flush you take a risk of slivering the adjoining veneered surface. To prevent damage place your thin straightedge in a position to protect the surface and force you to cut the overhang a fraction long. (15-10) Sand down the projecting edge. Some craftsmen say that trimming long and sanding flush also reduces chipping.

117

15-11. Increase central clamping pressure with scrap veneer slipped under wooden crossbearers

Another safeguard can be seen in the illustration. Notice that the knurled collar of the knife has been wrapped with masking tape. This trick saves veneer from scratches if you slide your knife against it. Tape also eliminates finger blisters when you do a lot of knife-cutting.

Increase clamping pressure. When you are clamping glued panels, and using wood crossbearers, pressure at the center is always lighter than around the edges, generally too light. Here is the quickest effective way to make sure of getting equal pressure at the center for good glue bond.

Under the crossbearers, at the center, slip a piece of scrap veneer, then tighten the clamps on the crossbearers. (15-11) Wood bearers become bowed at the ends and consequently slightly raised at the center when clamps are tightened. The veneer wedge overcomes this problem.

Use two veneer scraps, one on the other, instead of a single scrap if the panels are wide enough to need it and if your bearers are necessarily small because of small clamps. You can test center pressure by trying to wiggle the first scrap of veneer loose. Loosen clamps and insert another wedge if needed.

Cutting veneered panels apart. You get cleaner edges by cutting every panel to usable size before veneering it. You run unnecessary risk when you veneer a panel with the intention

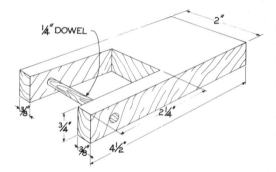

15-12. Make two clamp pads for each bar clamp you own. Install and leave them to protect work

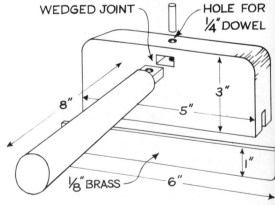

15-14. Veneer hammer is important homemade tool for applying adequate pressure to freshly glued veneer

118

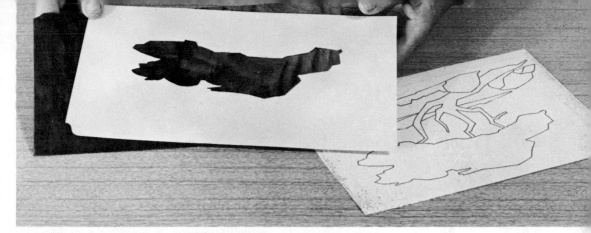

15-13. Where veneer figure is part of a design, use selector, made by cutting hole in cardboard

of cutting it into two or more smaller sizes. However, when you must cut down a veneered panel, this woodworking trick increases your chances of getting clean edges.

Whether you cut with a portable power saw or a table saw you must have a very sharp circular-saw blade. Of course a table saw is best. With either tool you cut with the best veneered face up. The blade always chips the underside more than the upside. Mark a pencil line on the underside. Bring the line up one edge and across the topside as well. On the underside, with sharp knife, score along the pencil line. This score must be fairly deep. In fact, at its best it should be a narrow V-groove. You need the accurate pencil line on the upside because this is your guideline for cutting.

If you own no power tools, there is a variation you can use. Score the underside as before. Clamp a wooden straightedge along the guideline on the topside. Of course you must use a perfectly true straightedge. Now run a sharp backsaw or dovetail saw along the straightedge. Saw through the panel in this way. This system is slow, but useful when you need it.

With any of these systems the underside veneer may chip slightly, but minimal underside chipping most times can be tolerated.

Clamp pads protect work. If you use bar clamps to hold edging or framing around veneered panels, make wooden pads to fit permanently, but loosely, on the bars, in front of each clamp jaw. (15-12) Follow the construction

details in the drawing, but make the notch in the pad of whatever size is required to fit your particular style of clamp. Glue a dowel across the open notch to hold the clamp pads. This device is far superior to loose pads.

Veneer selector. Chapter 7 described a device for locating the most appropriate area of veneer for a small requirement. It was a piece of cardboard with a rectangular opening cut in it.

A refinement of that type of viewer is the design selector shown here. (15-13) This selector is useful in craftwork where you are looking for figure detail that depicts its subject, such as the foliage of a tree. Butt walnut is being examined with a veneer selector cut from a piece of manila file folder.

Veneer hammer. One of the most vital steps in successful veneering takes place the minute you lay veneer on a glue-fresh panel. Unless you apply heavy pressure to assure over-all, even bond between veneer and panel, the veneer will blister.

To apply pressure most craftsmen use a roller, and it is an important tool to own, essential on small veneered panels. However, for larger work a few professionals know about and use the veneer hammer. If you want to own one, you will have to make it.

In chapter 6 you discovered a veneer hammer made by the author from a discarded floor buffer. In case you do not locate an old buffer, here is a working drawing (15-14) showing you how to make this important tool for your shop.

16. Pictorial veneering

As you discovered in preceding chapters of this book, veneering is a craft that reaches all the way from a set of simple gift coasters to veneered panels for major home improvements.

Projects for the demonstrations were selected because they involved the most useful techniques in modern veneering. You saw the methods, equipment, and materials you need to know about. Techniques were applied only to practical achievements. These same basic techniques of handling, selecting, cutting, and gluing veneers are equally helpful in the creative art of pictorial veneering, briefly introduced now.

Pictorial marquetry. Those who practice marquetry consider it the ultimate goal in artistic veneering. They appear to hurry from one cre-

ation to the next. Not that the work looks hurried. Quite the contrary. It looks painstaking and time-consuming. Their urgency is to become more involved with higher skills of artistry in their next picture. Not until you have tried this intriguing activity for yourself will you fully appreciate the truth of this observation.

Marquetry is the art of cutting and assembling pieces of veneer into a meaningful design and then gluing the one-piece assembly, which is held together with paper tape, onto a solid surface. Since we are concerned here with pictorial marquetry, the design in this case is a picture.

The intent of pictorial marquetry is to create a design that resembles, for instance, a country scene where birches grow. You do this by select-

Marquetry pictures like Sunday Morning and Birches are composed of numerous pieces of veneer which have been cut separately with a craft knife or hand fret saw. Cut pieces are placed in position, held to other pieces with gum tape until the assembly is complete and is glued to a solid mounting panel

At a marquetry exhibition sponsored by the Marquetry Society of America the two pictures shown here won top prizes: Cocker Spaniel by Anthony Guglielmo, and The Old Cowboy made by Dr. Albert Parker. Both are superb examples of veneer marquetry

Florida Everglades is another example of the reality that can be conveyed by veneers alone. In this marquetry creation it would be normal to use a few dyed woods especially to make colorful birds. All marquetry pictures start with a full-size pattern which is traced, one part at a time, onto veneer for cutting

ing woods of color and grain to depict each object in the scene. You might choose white holly or white bird's-eye maple for the sunny side of the birch trunk; harewood for the grey, mildly shaded side of the trunk; green poplar burl for foliage, and so on. Choosing woods to express your own artistic feeling for the subject is part of the rich reward to be found in marquetry.

The veneers you use in making marquetry pictures should be of equal thickness; that is, either 1/40 or 1/28. When necessary, you can combine two thicknesses of veneer in the same picture, usually leveling the surface by sanding,

you prepare them. Usually they are held together with paper tape until the entire assembly is ready for gluing onto a solid mounting board such as hardboard or flakeboard, which has been pre-cut to required size.

There are variations to this method, but this abbreviated account should be enough to guide you in a serious consideration of pictorial marquetry. As a beginner you will do well to avoid the temptation of making your first few patterns. There are tricks to pattern making that will not be obvious to you until you have made a few marquetry pictures. Starting with a professionally

Birds in Flight is a veneer craft pictur typical of the simplest type of desig Birds are separate overlays of lacewo on a stormy sky of gumwood and sea poplar. Stalking Tiger represents the of veneer craft carried one step furthe Tiger's body is satinwood. Stripes ebony, and head of zebrano cut separa ly and applied as overlays. Dried gra was a whimsical touch of the craftsm

or feathering the edges of the thicker veneers where they meet the thinner veneers.

The designs you use are subjects that can be expressed without a complication of detail, subjects having relatively simple perspective. Designs must be converted into line patterns. Patterns are traced, one part at a time, onto the selected piece of veneer. The veneer part is then cut to shape with a craft knife, or cut with a hand fret saw or power scroll saw. Each cutting method requires a different working procedure, and each method has its individual advantages.

Veneer parts are assembled piece by piece as

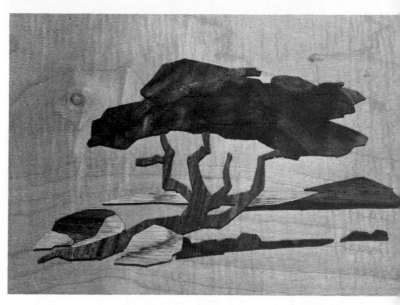

The Lone Cypress of Monterey is a sight most California travelers will recall. It represents one more step in the art of veneer craft. Here various parts join, but even this technique, while coming closer to marquetry, is not as exacting

designed kit is your best assurance of making a successful picture.

Readymade marquetry kits contain full-size patterns, colorful woods selected by wood experts, mounting board, and instructions. When you work from a kit, you do not have the freedom of choice in selecting which particular color of wood you prefer for various parts of the picture. On the other hand, you do not need an assortment of veneers on hand. In fact, with a kit, about all you need is a craft knife.

Pictorial veneering, simplified

A simpler variation of pictorial veneering is called veneer craft. It is easier than marquetry. In veneer craft you cut the design parts from veneer with craft knife or hand fret saw and assemble them on a mounting panel. You do not inlay the parts or fit them into a background to make a level assembly. Veneer craft is an overlay technique. Cut parts are glued on top of the panel and on top of each other when that is called for by the design.

The Stalking Tiger is an example of veneer craft. A full-size pattern of the tiger's body is traced on yellow-gold satinwood, and the veneer

is cut to shape. The body is glued onto a mounting board veneered with quartered walnut veneer or other dark wood. Stripes are traced to Macassar ebony and cut as separate pieces. Stripes are glued on top of the tiger's body. The face cut from zebrano, and the nose cut from teak, are overlaid in that order. Except for a stalk or two of dried grass, strictly optional, that completes the stalking tiger decorative panel. The simple procedure required no intricate cutting and fitting of parts.

Other illustrated examples of veneer craft shown here are The Lone Cypress of Monterey, and Birds in Flight. Notice that the birds are imposed on a veneered panel representing stormy sky and grey ocean. The choice of flecked lacewood for birds and swirly gumwood for stormy sky illustrates the way veneer can create the mood of a picture.

Veneer craft offers interesting possibilities in large, decorative wall panels based on a broad theme like Undersea World, composed of individual creatures of the deep, which by themselves would soon be within the ability of a newcomer to pictorial veneering.

17. Upgrading furniture with flexible veneer

There is now an easier way to turn unpainted chests, tables and cabinets into beautiful, expensive-looking furniture and to cover up battered surfaces of existing furniture. Introduction of an extra-thin real wood veneer only 1/64th of an inch thick with a tough non-removable backing has greatly simplified furniture veneering. A highly practical and increasingly popular use for the new flexible veneer is demonstrated here. The procedure shows a surprisingly easy way to make an elegant chest from an unpainted readymade two-drawer unit. Another demonstration shows a scarred and dented old table being renewed with flexible oak veneer.

When laid with contact glue as shown flexible veneer requires only a few simple tools, chiefly a craft knife and a long steel straightedge. Contact glue eliminates clamps and avoids the awkward and often impossible clamping setups for assembled furniture.

Most woodworkers are familiar with standard veneers measuring about 1/28" to 1/40" in thickness. But not very many have yet discovered the new, flexible 1/64" grade which is less brittle, easy to cut cleanly and

comes in much wider sheets. Standard widths are 18", 24" and 36". This means that a table top or chest surface can be covered with a single width without edge-jointing and gluing. It is available only in eight-foot rolls. You have a choice from fifteen or more of the most popular kinds of furniture woods such as cherry, curly maple, rift oak and English oak, teak, Honduras mahogany, Brazilian rosewood, East Indian rosewood, walnut, birch, Carpathian elm burl and other varieties.

To demonstrate the simple veneering procedure of applying flexible veneer to furniture an unpainted two-drawer chest was purchased from the mail-order catalog of J. C. Penney: Nite Table No. R804-2337A.

The basic requirement of a piece of furniture to be veneered is square edges. Rounded corners and molded edges cannot be veneered satisfactorily although the veneer can be bent around smooth edges to some extent. When you buy a piece of unfinished furniture look for flat surfaces and square edges. If you are resurfacing existing furniture — coffee table, chest, or cabinet — you may have no choice but to deal with

rounded edges. In such a case, strip the old finish from edges and refinish with stain to match the veneer you will lay on flat surfaces. If the old finish on flat surfaces is varnish, lacquer or wax, glue may not create a good enough bond unless you remove the old finish. Pitted surfaces and areas where old veneer has chipped off can be filled with non-shrinking powdered wood compound

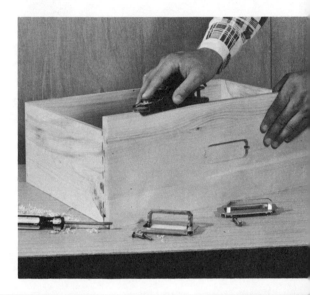

The unpainted chest bought from a mail-order catalog was chosen because it had square edges and would be easy to veneer. Flexible veneer will go over quarter-round edges, but cyma curves and other intricate molded edges are best avoided. Even square edges of unpainted readymade furniture require truing up with rasp and sandpaper

The drawer front is the only drawer surface to be veneered. Use a block plane to trim the edges for a loose fit. This precaution removes the possibility of a tight drawer and chipping veneer when humidity is high

125

Flexible veneer comes in eight-foot rolls and in widths 18", 24", 36". Determine best width for your project by making small layout, observing proper grain direction for each panel. Hold curling ends of roll with bricks in protective bags while cutting with craft knife against steel straightedge

Contact glue is easiest for furniture surfaces. It avoids difficult clamping. Pour small amount at a time on underside of veneer. Brush quickly. Repeat in 60 minutes. Treat chest side same

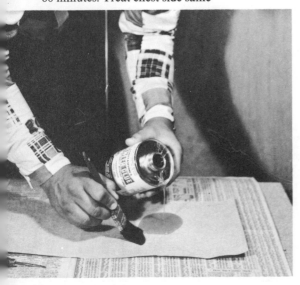

mixed with water and sanded smooth when hard.

Veneering techniques shown for the unfinished chest apply equally to your stripped down piece. Remove all hardware. To prepare the chest for veneer start by truing edges and corners with a cabinet rasp, file, block plane and sandpaper. Trim the top and side edges of each drawer front to establish a fairly loose fit. A tight drawer sets up a hazard to veneer edges in periods of high humidity.

Veneer only one surface at a time. The order of veneering will be this: first side, second side, top horizontal rail and top. Bottom and center rails come next and finally the vertical edges. This order is standard procedure to hide the most edge grain. The general principle is to veneer last that which you see first. If you are veneering the top of a coffee table, for example, lay the edges first, top last. Some experts lay edging last on the theory that the thin edges are not observed anyway.

Study the model to see how the veneer figure runs on each part of the chest. In accordance with good design grain runs vertically on the sides; from side to side on the top; horizontally on front rails; vertically on vertical front edges; and vertically on drawer fronts. Observe these rules when laying out the veneer roll before cutting.

It is not necessary to sand surfaces glassy-

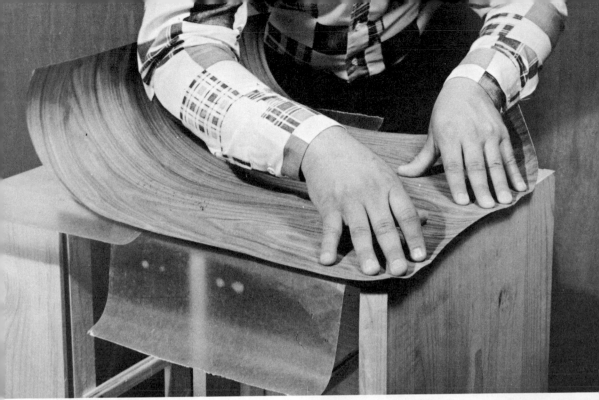

Slipsheet of wax paper prevents contact except along 1/4" exposed strip at starting edge. When veneer is perfectly aligned, allowing overhang at edges, withdraw slipsheet a little at a time while pressing veneer down with roller to assure firm overall contact. Trim overhang with knife

smooth as you would do prior to applying a fine finish. Glue bonding is better on a surface that has not been sanded that much. But don't leave a pitted or dented surface.

The roll of Brazilian rosewood for the two-drawer chest measured 24" wide by eight feet long. It could have provided all pieces for the chest which measures 21 1/2" high, 21 1/2" wide, 16 1/2" deep. For demonstration purposes we elected to cut drawer veneer from a roll of birch simply to show a variety of design treatment. If you foresee an opportunity to utilize the balance of the second roll, the extra cost is justified.

Before cutting any piece from the roll make a small-scale layout of all needed pieces with overhang allowances and figure running in the right direction. Double check to avoid errors in cutting.

The first piece to cut from the roll is for one side. From one long edge of this piece you also get top and bottom rails. Lay the veneer, figure side up, on a clean, smooth cutting surface like a panel of particle board or hardboard, but not fir which is too uneven for knife cutting. Cutting from the figure side makes a cleaner cut on that side. Measure off a piece about 1 1/2" longer than the chest panel. This allows 3/4" overhang at each end. On smaller pieces allow less overhang. Lay a straightedge on the veneer as a cutting guide. A 24" steel square is a better straightedge than a strip of wood. Hold the flexing roll with weights such as bricks in produce bags which prevent scratches. An X-acto No. 11 blade makes the cleanest cut. Use only a fresh blade and sharpen or replace it often when cutting veneer.

The glue to use is contact type which requires no clamping. The newest contacts are non-flammable, an important improvement. One called Non-Flammable Veneer Glue was used here. Never use water soluble contact adhesive on veneer. It will curl the veneer. Contact glue must be spread on both surfaces to be joined. Lay the veneer sheet upside down on layered newspapers which can be removed a sheet at a time as it becomes glue-smeared. Pour a small amount and spread quickly, brushing outward across edges and as much as possible only in one direction. Spread a fairly heavy coat. Don't keep dabbing at the wet surfaces with your brush even when bubbles appear. The second coat will cover remaining thin areas.

Spread glue on the chest surface. Keep glue-spread surfaces far apart. If they touch, they will weld. Allow 60 minutes for the glue to dry. Apply a second coat in the same way and again wait 60 minutes.

Top photograph. Last edges to be veneered are side edges of case. Strips hide edge grain of sides. Figure runs vertically to support illusion of solid-panel sides. Handle holes were veneered over. Now feel your way around edges for path of knife to remove veneer. Sand trimmed edges. Stroke lengthwise, never across veneer edge

Use the slipsheet method when laying veneer on the chest. Wax paper was used here. Some craftsmen use heavy brown paper. Place the wax paper about 1/4" back from the starting edge of the chest. Align the veneer sheet accurately with about 3/4" extending as overhang. When the veneer is accurately aligned all the way to the other end, finger-press veneer against the exposed 1/4" strip of chest. Rub the veneer down along this edge. Press hard, but don't press heavily where the slipsheet is underneath or the veneer will adhere somewhat to the paper. Pull the slipsheet so as to expose another glue area about an inch wide. Rub down the veneer and apply fairly heavy pressure with a roller, always rollering in the grain direction. Crosswise rollering could split the veneer. Continue to withdraw the slipsheet and roller the veneer to the end. Be careful with the roller at all overhanging edges. Roller more to assure perfect contact in all areas. If you feel a blister, roller the area even more, always in grain direction. Set the work aside for an hour while the glue is hardening.

Trim overhanging edges of veneer with your craft knife. Place the veneered surface on a smooth cutting surface, brushed clean. Make several passes with the knife instead of trying to cut through in one pass. Let the knife ride against the edge of the chest as a guide, but be careful not to nick the edge.

Now, using very fine or worn sandpaper on a block, stroke gently along the cut edge of veneer to remove any unevenness of the knife cut. Don't work the block back and forth across the veneer edge. Continue to lay one piece at a time in the order suggested earlier. When you are trimming the overhang of the top, be extra careful not to nick the veneered sides.

This chest had inset handles on the sides and drawer front. We ignored the handle recesses and laid veneer over them. Now it is time to cut an opening in the veneer so the handles can be replaced. You can feel the depression through the veneer and can make the cuts by feeling your way along. Remove loose veneer and trim around the opening. A perfect edge is not essential because hardware covers the trimmed edge.

Only the front of the drawer is to be veneered. Other surfaces can be prefinished with stain and lacquer, or clear lacquer or sealer alone as a protective coat. Polyurethane clear varnish was the only finish applied to veneered surfaces because of a preference for a satin finish that accentuates the beauty of natural wood.

Front panel is only drawer surface veneered. Coat other surfaces with clear sealer. Trim veneer overhang with knife. Fit drawer into case. Veneered edges can still be lightly sanded for loose fit

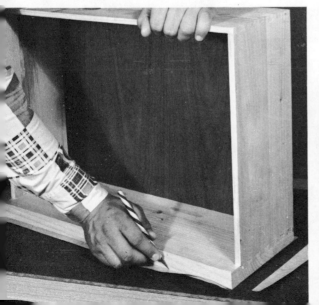

Veneering old furniture surfaces

Wide sheets of flexible veneer are the home restorer's best friend. Battered table tops, square edges, even square legs such as those on once-popular mission oak furniture are readily covered up with handsome varieties of flexible veneer. Oak is being laid with contact glue on the table below. At right is an example of surface preparation of a drop leaf removed from an early tavern table. Its many holes and dents were packed with powdered wood compound mixed with water, allowed to harden and sanded smooth. Never lay veneer on a pitted or bumpy surface.

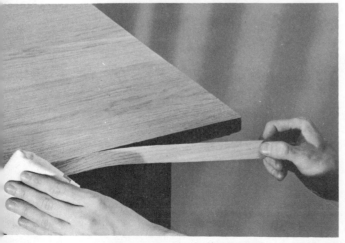

18. Making a multi-colored inlaid chessboard

When you think of making a chessboard, why spend the time on a conventional walnut and maple pattern? Instructions given here show you how to make a distinctive one-of-a-kind multi-colored chessboard. All light squares are curly maple. A three-foot piece is more than enough. Dark squares are many different kinds, the richest colors and most interesting figures you can find.

The technique used here involves the making of veneer strips 2" wide, light strips and dark strips. You do not cut individual 2" squares. This is the easy way to compose a checker assembly. Provide a cutting board by attaching quarter-round molding along one edge of smooth particle board. (18-3)

From scrap vinyl countertop material accurately cut a 2" gauge strip about 18" long. With the aid of this gauge cut 2" veneer strips and assemble them, alternating light and dark, with veneer tape. Make pads of three strips and pads of five. Next, turn the pads a quarter turn and cut 2" strips. Now you have pads composed of three checker squares and pads of five squares. The squares are still taped. Strips do not have to be the same length, but you must cut enough of the same length to make pads of three strips consisting of two darks and one light. (18-6) And cut enough of the same length to make pads of five strips consisting of three

Chessboard panel is 3/8 particle board 18x18 veneered both sides before veneer squares are laid

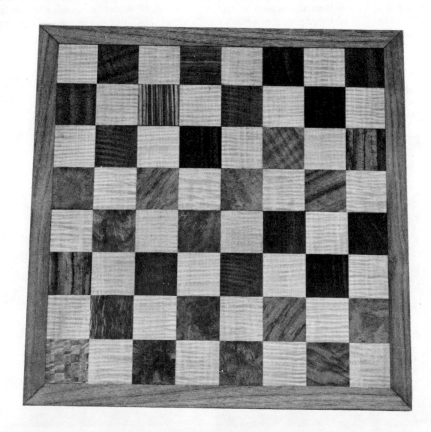

Your unique chessboard deserves a set of veneer chessmen. Glue dark veneer both sides of 1/8" wo Light wood for second set. Cut with fret saw. Patterns from *Veneer Craft for Everyone*

Above, 18-2, and 18-3 below show leftover walnut scrap with one straight edge against molding on cutting board. Vinyl gauge 2" wide guides veneer saw in cutting this veneer and all other pieces exactly the same width. Size of scrap determined its usable length of 4 1/4. Cut one more dark and one light, same length. These three pieces will be taped together, darks outside, as in top left photo on next page. Cut more darks and lights to form 3-piece and 5-piece pads. Tape-assembled pads are cut crosswise under vinyl gauge to produce checker-square pads

Above, typical assortment of 4 x 9 veneers from which a wide selection of dark squares can be cut. Below, 18-4, stroke cut edge across flat sandpaper sheet. 18-5, test squareness of cut strips

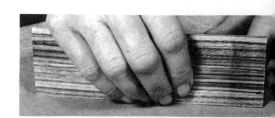

18-6 above shows two darks outside and one light in middle being taped tightly edge to edge. This pad is 6 1/4 long and will yield three checker pads 3 squares wide when cut crosswise under vinyl gauge. 18-7 at upper right shows cutting 5-strip assembly, lights outside, so it will yield three checker pads 5 squares wide. 18-8, at right, is partial assortment of pads produced. One 5-piece and one 3-piece pad combine to form one full row for chessboard. Below, pads are being trial-assembled to select best combinations of 5's and 3's

lights and two darks. (18-7) Be sure to assemble as shown: pads of three strips have darks outside; pads of five strips have lights outside and in the middle. You need eight checker pads of five squares; and eight checker pads of three squares. Your chessboard requires eight rows, each formed with one 3-piece checker pad and one 5-piece checker pad. In trial assembly (18-9) you have plenty of optional combinations of 3's and 5's to form a row. Start the top row with a light square at left, dark at right. Bottom row must have dark at left, light at right. Keep switching pad locations until you have no dark squares touching dark squares of the same kind of veneer.

Original 2" strips can be cut 4 1/4 long to produce two identical pads; or 6 1/4 long to produce three identical pads. If you cut longer strips, you end up with too many identical pads for good makeup.

For safest handling of precious pads, assemble two full-width rows into one pad. (18-10) Lay the double-row pad with contact Veneer Glue. Use slipsheet method. (18-11) Edges of completed checker assembly need squaring. Add veneer border strips. Glue veneer trim on panel edges. Apply polyurethane varnish. Rub first coat with 240 sandpaper, second coat with pumice and rubbing compound.

18-10 at top shows checker-square pads of 3's and 5's being taped to form two full-width rows for chessboard panel. 18-11, double row, coated underneath with contact glue (not water soluble type) being laid on glue-spread panel, wax paper slipsheet between to avoid premature contact. Moisten and peel tape from final assembly. 18-12, edges of assembled chess squares being trimmed square. Veneer border, glued and mitered

19. Techniques for veneering trays and gift boxes

When you put your knowledge of veneering to work on useful projects for your home the rewards are substantial. Serving trays of distinctive design are good examples of projects that generate frequent admiration. The matched veneer tray shown here in spite of its elegant appearance is not at all hard to make. There are two ways to make it. You can purchase a readymade 4-piece matched crotch walnut face measuring 15 x 30 and cut it to 15 x 23 which is a practical size for a tray. Or you can make up a veneer face by cutting and edge-gluing any exotic veneer of your choice. Techniques demonstrated in earlier chapters show how to lay a veneer face on a stable panel of particle board or hardboard. Be sure also to lay veneer on the back of the panel to reduce possible warping tendency.

One of the best ways to make a close-fit-ting joint is illustrated. (19-1) Select the area of best figure in each sheet of veneer. The sheets you are working with, if purchased at the same time, will be consecutive sheets and will have matching figure. Mark the amount you want to remove from joining edges in order to bring the interesting matching figure of each sheet the same distance from the edge. Lay one sheet on top of the other so the waste area at the edge overlaps the waste area of the sheet beneath it. Place your steel straightedge along the cutting line and use a veneer saw to cut through both sheets without moving veneer or straightedge even the slightest amount. The resulting edges, having been cut at the same time will fit together perfectly. Bring the pieces together tightly at the joint. Lay veneer tape on the face side. Roller the tape hard. That's the way to make it stick best. Turn the assembly over. Flex

open the joint very slightly. Run a stream of white glue into the open joint. Wipe off surplus glue. Glue smear will be hidden because this is the underside. Cover the glued joint with wax paper, place between caul boards and lay weights on top for overnight.

Make the tray frame from handsome picture frame molding. Selecting molding that flares outward and upward. Cut miters at corners. Glue, assemble and clamp the frame. Always complete a frame by itself. Never assemble around a panel. Slip the panel, now veneered on two sides, into the frame. (19-2) The flared picture frame molding selected for this tray allows good finger grip without the encumbrance of handles.

19-1. One cut through both sheets at same time for best joint. 19-2. Frame is pre-assembled

Veneering a circular plaque

This demonstration shows a simple way to position an oversize veneer face on a circular plaque and have the veneer design accurately centered. The same aligning trick can be used when mounting a square or rectangular face. The problem confronting the craftworker is to center the veneer design when laying it blind. A readymade veneer face of The Great Seal of the United States is used in the demonstration.

Start the procedure by laying the seal veneer, face side down, on a smooth work surface. Lay the circular mounting disc on top of the veneer. Center the two elements by having an equal overhanging margin of veneer all around. Trace around the disc with a pencil. (19-3) Now drive three finishing nails through the overhanging veneer. Nails must be held tightly against the mounting disc. (19-4) Nail holes in waste veneer will be trimmed off. Remove the disc and coat the veneer with contact glue. (19-5) Also coat the mounting disc. Use two coats spaced an hour apart, following gluing instructions given earlier. When glue on both surfaces is ready for contact carefully drop the disc, glue side down, onto the glue-spread surface of the veneer. (19-6) Use a mallet and wood block to apply overall pressure. (19-7) Withdraw nails. Trim overhang with a craft knife. (19-8) Scrape off veneer tape still remaining on the veneer face. Moisten sparingly small areas at a time. Scrape cautiously and patiently. (19-9) Attach brass gallery around the mounting panel. (19-10) Add rubber feet underneath to protect table surfaces from the brass gallery and to raise the tray for an easy finger grip. *Continued*

19-3. Center disc on veneer face. Trace around it.
19-4. Drive nails against disc into waste veneer.
19-5. Brush contact glue on veneer and on disc.

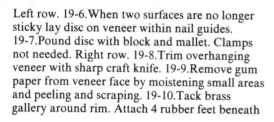

Left row. 19-6. When two surfaces are no longer sticky lay disc on veneer within nail guides. 19-7. Pound disc with block and mallet. Clamps not needed. Right row. 19-8. Trim overhanging veneer with sharp craft knife. 19-9. Remove gum paper from veneer face by moistening small areas and peeling and scraping. 19-10. Tack brass gallery around rim. Attach 4 rubber feet beneath

Decorating small boxes with veneer

Unpainted boxes sold in most craft stores invite imaginative decoration with colorful veneers. Most veneers are sold in three-foot lengths. One sheet yields more than enough to cover any box in this demonstration. The five boxes shown in this chapter represent a variety of veneering techniques. In each example the entire box is covered with veneer, but final appearance is widely different.

Start by removing the drive hinges. Obtain screw hinges which are easier to install when the box is veneered. You now work with two separated parts, compartment and lid. Cut an oversize veneer square for each panel. Overhang is trimmed off with a craft knife

after gluing. Edges are then gently sanded. Contact glue eliminates awkward clamping. Yellow glue is acceptable if you provide caul strips of proper size and work with small C-clamps. To hide veneer edges as much as possible the order of veneering is back, sides, front and top. Glue one panel at a time. Trim overhang before starting an adjacent panel.

One of the most useful techniques demonstrated is the simple method of inlaying. Sunburst, eagle and initial insets are traced on the veneer panel for the top. A precise opening is knife-cut and the inset is edge-glued and filled before the panel is glued to the box. The jewel box shows inlay banding included.

Savings bond box, African cherry veneer. Eagle inlay set in place before top veneer was laid

Music box covered with curly maple illustrates simplified inlay method. Opening for initial is cut in top veneer and packed with mix of glue and matching sawdust filler on underneath side

Jewel box covered with padauk utilizes the simple inlay method and shows how to include decorative banding

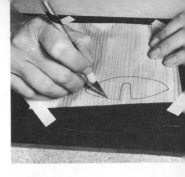

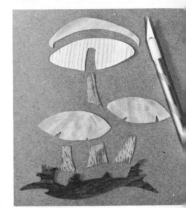

Recipe box holds about 400 cards. Bought readymade as all boxes in this book. Covered with benge veneer. Top decorated with knife-cut veneer. Mushroom and frog design from Creative Veneer Craft book

Game box holds chips, checkers, or two decks of cards. Owl panel is readymade. Sides and front are covered with crotch walnut which was cut so veneer figure flows uninterrupted from lower section to lid. Below, oversize cut parts and method of laying glue-fresh box lid, centered, on pencil-outlined owl veneer

INDEX

Parquetry veneer designs make interesting
lay-ons for covering battered table tops. Here
three-inch squares of koa veneer were laid
with grain of adjacent squares turned